SELF-LOVE   vs.

"Is motivated towards self-advantage in thought, word, and deed."	"Is motivated in every thought, word and action by love of God, and neighbor as self."
"Sees only other's faults, not his own. Considers himself on the right path – perhaps even humble and virtuous."	"Sees himself full of imperfections. Is always seeking to be perfected through love. Considers everyone more humble and holy than himself."
"Holds a checklist in his heart of every wrong perpetrated against him."	"Imitates Divine Mercy as best he can. Is compassionate and forgiving."
"Is quick to anger and stands vigil over his own rights, making certain they are not transgressed."	"Is patient. Takes note of others' needs and concerns."
"Hangs on to his own opinions refusing to surrender to another viewpoint."	"Offers his own opinions but listens to others and lends them equal merit with his own."
"Takes pride in his own achievements. May even take pride in his spiritual progress."	"Realizes all things proceed from God; that without God he is capable of no good thing. All good comes from grace."
"Sees himself and the world as the be-all/end-all. His only pleasure is thus achieved through the world."	"Takes joy in storing up heavenly treasure: in growing closer to God and deeper in holiness. Knows the difference between earthly pleasures and spiritual joy."
"Uses the goods of the world to satisfy self."	"Uses the goods of the world to satisfy quest for holiness."
"Objects to every cross. Sees trials as a curse. Resents others' good fortune."	"Surrenders to the cross through love as Jesus did. Sees crosses as a grace to be used to convert others."
"Prays only for himself and his own needs."	"Prays for all in need."
"Cannot accept God's Will. Becomes bitter over trials."	"Accepts God's Will with a loving heart even when difficult."

(Given to Maureen Sweeney-Kyle by Blessed Mother on August 18, 1997)

June 17, 2002
Conversation with Divine Love

"I am your Jesus, born Incarnate. Child, I created you in the womb as I create each one to be a reflection of My Flame of Divine Love. I alone know how to call forth the inner beauty of the jewel of your soul. With My own Hand I chisel away the rough nature which influences the beauty I created. You often do not recognize My tools, though you feel their sharpness. My tools are temptation and trials. Every test of virtue that you pass becomes a new facet on the face of the jewel of your heart."

"Finally, when I am finished, I look with eagerness to bring My jewel into Paradise—to reveal My handiwork amongst the angels and the saints. The perfect setting awaits the jewels that I refine. It is My Mother's Heart. Within Her Immaculate Heart every jewel reflects the elegance of the Flame of My Fire of Divine Love. It is My call to each soul."

Lessons

on

The Virtues

Second Edition

Archangel Gabriel Enterprises, Inc.

The first edition of this booklet published in 1999 contained messages received by the Visionary, Maureen Sweeney-Kyle, as lessons from Jesus on the virtues. This second edition has been expanded to include a selection of messages from Jesus, God the Father, Our Lady, St. Thomas Aquinas and other saints, on the virtuous life and the virtues themselves. All messages are posted on our website at http://www.holylove.org.

Current Canonical Explanation:

Response to Apparitions and Visionaries

for Roman Catholics

Since the abolition of Canon 1399 and 2318 of the former Code of Canon Law by Paul VI in AAS58 (1966) page 1186, publications about new apparitions, revelation, prophecies, miracles, etc., have been allowed to be distributed and read by the faithful without the express permission of the Church, providing that they contain nothing which contravenes faith and morals. This means, no imprimatur is necessary.

The Discernment of Visionaries and Apparitions Today

by Albert J. Hebert, S.M., Page III

Published by:
©1999, 2007 Archangel Gabriel Enterprises Inc.
Elyria, OH 44039   All rights reserved
First edition published 1999. Second edition 2007

CONTENTS

About the Apparitions

Since 1985, Jesus and Blessed Mother have been appearing to Maureen Sweeney-Kyle on an almost daily basis and have given her a series of missions to accomplish.

1986–1990
OUR LADY, PROTECTRESS OF THE FAITH*

1990–1993
PROJECT MERCY
(*Nationwide Anti-Abortion Rosary Crusades*)

1993–Present
The combined Revelations of **MARY, REFUGE OF HOLY LOVE** and the **CHAMBERS OF THE UNITED HEARTS**. In 1993, Our Lady asked that this Mission be known as **HOLY LOVE MINISTRIES**.

*NOTE: On August 28, 1988, Our Lady came as "Guardian of the Faith" to Visionary, Patricia Talbot, of Cuenca, Ecuador, in South America. In 1991, the Bishops of Ibarra and Guayaquil in Ecuador approved the movement which contains the name "Guardian of the Faith" and thus implicitly the title.

Visionary:

Maureen Sweeney-Kyle is a very shy, timid and frail housewife and grandmother. She grew up and still resides in the Cleveland, Ohio area with her husband. In 1993, Our Lady began **Holy Love Ministries** and then requested that the Ministry procure property for a shrine in Lorain County, Ohio. This was accomplished in 1995 (115 acres) and is now known as **Maranatha Spring & Shrine**, home of **Holy Love Ministries**, an Ecumenical Lay Apostolate to make known to the world the Chambers of the United Hearts.

Spiritual Director:

Over the past twenty years, Maureen has had four spiritual directors who have been experts in Marian Theology.

On the joyful occasion of the visit by the visionary, Maureen Sweeney-Kyle, with Pope John Paul II in August of 1999. Her husband, Don *(lower right)*, the Late Archbishop Gabriel Ganaka *(top left)*, and Rev. Frank Kenney, her Spiritual Director (1994-2004) *(top center)*, accompanied her on the visit.

The Stairway of Holiness

March 24, 1999
VISION OF THE STAIRWAY

Jesus showed me a big staircase in a vision. It reached up to the sky. He comes. He says, "I am your Jesus, born Incarnate. I have come to discuss the stairway with you. It is, indeed, the Stairway of Holiness that leads to Heaven. Each step represents a virtue. The mortar between the bricks [it is made of bricks] represents Holy Love, as love binds all virtues together. You will notice that the first step is very great compared to the others. It can only be mounted with sincere effort and choice of free will. It is humility. None of the other steps [virtues] are attainable without humility of heart. The soul needs to really <u>submit</u> to that step. It is not mounted through false pretense."

"Look at the railing along side the steps. This is what the soul clings to in order to stay on the staircase. Do you understand what it represents? It is simplicity. Through simplicity the soul keeps its focus on God in the present moment."

"See the angels I have given you to help you climb." [There are angels along side the stairs.] "Do not be afraid of falling. Once you begin, the angels will assist you."

"The door at the top of the stairs is the doorway to My Heart—the door of Divine Love."

"I will bless your efforts in making this known."

August 24, 2006
EACH STEP IS A VIRTUE

St. Thomas Aquinas says: "Praise be to Jesus."

"You are asking in your heart how each virtue can be a separate step on the Stairway to Holiness. It is true—all the virtues must come together in the soul in order to achieve perfection and harmony with God's Divine Will; however, not all virtue is obtained at once. Virtue is a combination of the free will in cooperation with the graces received through the Heart of Mary."

"In order to increase in virtue, the soul must first acknowledge his shortcomings in the virtues. Then he needs to pray to overcome these faults. For instance, if the soul is given over to impatience, then he needs to pray for the grace to become patient; practice patience, and Our Heavenly Mother will gradually give him a strong gift of the virtue of patience."

"So you see why self-knowledge is so important. Without it, the soul cannot continue his journey into the Divine Will. Every virtue has its counter in sin, which battles against conformity to the Divine Will. Each soul has its own individual battle to fight—its own flaws in virtue—its own strengths and weaknesses. Every step towards perfection in virtue is opposed by evil. Satan cringes at the thought of personal holiness. This is why it is important to pray for yourself, as well as others."

May 16, 2000
EACH STEP TAKES HUMILITY AND COURAGE

"I am your Jesus, born Incarnate. You know that I love you. I have loved you from the beginning of time and will love you for all eternity, just as I love each soul. Through the depth of My Love, I come to ask you to pray in this way for all humanity: Pray that souls have the courage to live this Message of Holy and Divine Love. Just as the first step on the Stairway of Holiness requires great effort, so does the first step in living these Messages require great effort. Both of these steps are one. They are humility. Without humility the soul does not have the courage to look into his own heart and discover his faults. Without this self-knowledge he cannot move forward in holiness. Self-knowledge and the acceptance of it is the doorway to Holy Love and the first step to the Chambers of My Heart. Such humility requires courage. It is much easier to live in compromise and think all is well and that you are as holy as you should be. It takes humility and courage to surrender to the truth."

"This humility and courage must surround you and follow you. It must lead you up the Stairway of Holiness. For the deeper the soul progresses in the Chambers of My Heart, the more he is aware of little flaws that block his way to perfection—to union."

"Now you will please make this known."

May 22, 1999
SELF-SURRENDER MOVES YOUR FEET UP THE STAIRS

"I am your Jesus, Divine Love, born Incarnate. I have come to explain to you the fullness of My call, which is self-surrender....Self-surrender is the key that unlocks the door to My Heart and to Divine Providence....Your self-surrender is what moves your feet up the staircase of holiness..."

The Virtuous Life

Introduction

January 16, 1999
JESUS ON THE VIRTUOUS LIFE

Jesus comes, His Heart exposed. He says: "I am Jesus, the Word Incarnate. I have come to help you realize the importance of a virtuous life. It is through the virtues you come into Holy Love—the Immaculate Heart. It is through a deepening of the virtues you come into My Heart—Divine Love."

"Understanding the virtues helps you to see where you are failing in them. The virtuous soul is at peace. If Satan tries to attack such a one, peace is regained quickly. The virtuous soul knows himself. He knows his weaknesses and he tries sincerely to overcome them. Virtue and holiness go hand in hand. The one truly advancing in holiness does not present himself as one who must be accommodated and placated. Rather, he is the loving servant of all. He never flaunts his spirituality nor aspires for recognition, but is content to remain in the background. Thus hidden, he does not set himself up as judge of others, but works on the virtues in his own life."

"I help those who call upon Me. I am inviting each one into My Divine Love. Come to Me."

January 1, 2007
ST. THOMAS AQUINAS ON THE VIRTUOUS LIFE

St. Thomas Aquinas says: "Praise be to Jesus."

"Today, on this royal feast day, I have come to expound on the virtuous life. [It is the Feast of the Mother of God.]

"Every virtue springs from the Heart of God because every virtue is God's Holy and Divine Will. Knowing this, you must understand that the more the soul imitates Divine Mercy and Divine Love, the deeper the virtues in his heart, for Mercy and Love are the essence of the Divine Will."

"It is like this—God's Divine Will can be likened to the force that pushes water out of a fountain. This force burgeons forth, spraying the water up and out for everyone to see and admire. The water in this analogy, of course, is the virtues. In the virtuous person, all of the virtues are visible for others to see and admire. The fountain, of course, does not look at itself and say, 'Look at me. I'm so beautiful.

I am impressing everyone.' In true virtue, the soul must be just as detached from his spiritual strengths as the water in the fountain, not regarding whom or how much he impresses others. It is false virtue that tries to impress. True virtue springs only from Mercy and Love with a Holy Indifference as to the effect on those around him."

The Virtuous Heart

March 13, 2000
A VIRTUOUS HEART

"I am your Jesus, born Incarnate. I have come to help you understand that the virtues are the threads which weave together the fabric of God's Will in the soul. Moreover, your self-will is the needle which pulls the thread of this fabric in place. Therefore, understand that a virtuous heart is enclothed in a rich fabric of God's Divine Will."

July 22, 2002
TRUE VIRTUE TRANSFORMS THE HEART

Jesus and Blessed Mother are here with Their Hearts exposed. Blessed Mother says: "Praise be to Jesus."

Jesus: "I am your Jesus, born Incarnate. My brothers and sisters, tonight I encourage you to allow transforming virtue to come into your hearts. Such virtue can only take root in a heart that is humble and full of Holy Love. All other virtue that does not transform you into My Likeness is false."

"Tonight We are blessing you with the Blessing of Our United Hearts."

July 10, 1999
THE HEART IS LIKE A HOUSE

"I am your Jesus, born Incarnate. Today I invite you to see that each heart can be likened to a little house. The door is free will. The owner of the house can admit either good or evil. What the householder allows in is also what comes out in the world around him."

"If the little house is a virtuous dwelling—a house of holiness— the bricks and mortar it is constructed with will be Holy Love, Holy Humility. These are the two that surround all the other virtues—unite them and make them strong."

"Without love and humility other virtues cannot truly dwell in the heart; there is no structure with which to hold them there: self-love assumes the role of the brick and mortar; false virtue—which is for show—envelops the heart."

"This is why you must measure the worth of every present moment according to Holy Love—Holy Humility."

"Surrender to Me and I will assist you."

January 28, 2006 — Feast of St. Thomas Aquinas
THE HEART VS. THE SPIRIT

St. Thomas Aquinas says: "Praise be to Jesus."

"You have been asking Heaven, in your heart, the difference between the heart and the spirit. The heart is the vessel which holds all virtue or lack of virtue. The spirit is the essence of what is in the heart. Let me explain it to you in this way."

"If the heart was an exotic perfume, the spirit would be the fragrance of the perfume. Or, if the heart was a beautiful garden with a lovely array of plants and birds, babbling brooks and more, the spirit would be the peace that one feels walking through the garden."

"The spirit is the invisible aura around a person that decries what is in the person's heart. Thus, you say, 'He is a joyful person—a peaceful person.' Or, on the other hand, 'He is an angry person,' and so on. It is always free will which determines what is in the heart and, therefore, what is reflected in the spirit."

"Just as a mirror portrays truthfully all that is placed before it, the spirit reflects truthfully what is in the heart."

"A fine wine cannot exude a false bouquet; neither can the spirit exude anything but what is contained in the heart."

The Value of the Present Moment

June 15, 1999
SINGULAR GRACE

Jesus comes. His Heart is exposed. His Heart seems to 'open' and a great light comes out of it. He says, "I am Jesus, born Incarnate. I have come to invite you to understand the great moment of grace every present moment affords."

"In the present moment the soul chooses either salvation or condemnation, for with God there is no half measure. The lukewarm I will spew from My Mouth. If you are not for Me, you are against Me."

"Be holy in the present moment for the present moment is a gift from Me to you and it will never be given again. Each moment I give you is singular in its grace, its opportunity, its call. You will find the Will of God for you in every moment by seeking and living the Holy Love Message. For to love Me is to know Me. To love Me is to trust in Me. Give to Me the favor of your surrender. I will give you so much more. Do not waste the moment that surrounds you and embraces you."

June 25, 1999
AFFECTS FUTURE MOMENTS

"Let us begin with this dictation. I am your Jesus, born of the flesh. Just as Holy Love sanctifies the mundane moment and makes it worthy in the eyes of God, come to see that the deeper you go into the Flame of Holy Love in the present moment, the more grace I will pour through My Mother's Heart into all your future moments. The more you practice the virtues in the present, the easier the virtues will come to you in the future."

"Therefore, understand that Satan wants to discourage every effort in Holy Love in the present moment. The devil knows all too well that each present moment affects the future. This is why you must pray and recommend your hearts to My Love and Mercy in the present. Satan fears any effort in Holy Love. He knows that Holy Love is his archenemy, as it is the Heart of My Mother."

"If you desire great grace and many favors in your lives, turn your hearts over to Me now in the present. Abundant is My Provision upon those who trust Me in such a way."

"Make it known that I may bless you."

July 19, 1999
SURRENDER TO LOVE

"Dearest child, I am your Jesus, born Incarnate. I have come to help you understand the value of the present moment. I do not ask of you heroic deeds and pious acts in each and <u>every</u> present moment as a means of salvation. I do ask your surrender to the Law of Love. This is the way of reconciliation with your Creator. Mankind has lost sight of this truth. I have come today to renew every heart in a commitment to Holy Love."

"Take for instance one Hail Mary. If it is recited with a loving heart it brings with it the power to convert a soul, to stop a war, to deliver a soul from purgatory, even to change the future of the world. See then that the love in your heart when you pray determines the power of the prayer."

"Suppose you were to make a great sacrifice but with much tepidity. I would honor a small, hidden sacrifice done with much Holy Love so much more!"

"If you were to surrender to Me everything you own, but did so begrudgingly or with much flamboyance and show, I would not honor such a sacrifice as much as one Hail Mary offered in the quiet of your heart with much love."

"Do not lose sight of this truth. Do not be confounded by how much you give Me, but always give with love. This is the key to accomplishing much good and to staying within the Divine Will of My Father. Make it known."

December 16, 2005
ETERNAL VALUE

St. Thomas Aquinas comes. He says: "Praise be to Jesus."

"I have come to help you understand how to make the present moment valuable in God's Eyes. You give the present moment eternal value when you hold the love of God in your heart. This is not always on a conscious level; that is to say, thinking, 'I love you, Jesus.' Rather, it is a love rooted in the heart—in the spirit—that motivates thought, word and deed."

"The present moment that is spent on impatience, unforgiveness, anger or any emotion that opposes love of God is wasted. This is why the soul needs to practice every virtue for love of God. Never try to impress others with your holiness. This arises from false virtue. Ask the holy angels to keep you on course. **When you arise in the morning, ask the angels to flood your heart with love of God and neighbor.** Do not underestimate the power of this practice. The Triune God desires that you have every advantage to lead you towards sanctity."

February 26, 2007
ACCEPT GOD'S WILL

"I am your Jesus, born Incarnate."

"I have come to help the world to see that My Father's Divine Will is in every present moment. Thus, His Perfect Will presents both cross and victory. It is the way in which each soul <u>accepts</u> the Father's Will in each present moment, that determines the amount of grace that pours forth from My Mother's Heart in assistance."

"If the soul begrudgingly accepts My Father's Will, Heaven is more reluctant to assist him. Perhaps he cannot accept, at all, the Will of God. This leads to an unforgiving heart and eventually bitterness. Perhaps the soul takes pride in some type of victory My Father allows, not acknowledging God's role in the triumph. This attitude fans the flames of self-love which leads away from trustful surrender."

"So you see, it is the disposition of the heart in every present moment that either leads the soul closer or farther away from living in the Divine Will."

The Spiritual Journey through the Chambers

January 3, 2000
THE CHAMBERS OF THE UNITED HEARTS

"Child, I am your Jesus, born Incarnate. Understand that the Chambers of My Heart are the embrace of Divine Love and the fulfillment of the Divine Will. The soul cannot mount to perfection apart from My Heart. Every virtue is rooted in this Divine Heart. Every

14

grace comes through the Heart of My Mother, which is the First Chamber—the prelude—to My Heart. Only united to Me can a soul reach salvation. Please make this known."

April 25, 2001
THE SPIRITUAL JOURNEY

"I am your Jesus, born Incarnate. I have come to help you see once again the importance of the present moment. It is in the grace of the present moment that you must make the journey into the Chambers of My Heart. In the present moment then, is your perfection in every virtue and your conformity to the Divine Will."

"Understand that every present moment is an opportunity of growth. Every present moment is a test of virtue. It is only in the test that virtue is perfected. If you desire to be patient, you will be given opportunities to be patient and, therefore, grow in patience. If you desire humility, you will be humbled—and so it goes with every virtue. The challenge in virtue is proof of its existence or absence in the soul."

"But if the soul misses the present moment, he also misses the opportunity for growth and perfection. See then, that the Second Chamber opens the way to the Third, Fourth and Fifth Chambers of My Heart."

March 8, 2003
PERFECTION OF THE VIRTUES

St. Thomas Aquinas says: "Praise be to Jesus. I have come to help you see that all the grace obtained in one Chamber of the United Hearts is carried into the next Chamber and deepened. In other words the soul enters the First Chamber and is purified of his iniquity through Holy Love. When he enters the Second Chamber—holiness in the present moment—the purification he experienced in the First Chamber abides with him and continues. As he seeks to be holy in the present moment, he is even more aware of the slightest fault or iniquity, and strives to overcome them."

"Gradually, the soul is drawn into the Third Chamber which is perfection of the virtues. The virtues are deepened through an awareness of imperfections in the present moment—the First and Second Chambers. And so it goes until the Kingdom of God—the Kingdom of the Divine Will—is established within the soul itself through union with the Divine Will."

"So you see, this spiritual journey is like building a house—a spiritual refuge—within the human heart. One block builds upon another until the Kingdom of the Divine Will is enthroned with the heart itself."

"Make this known."

January 27, 2000
THE SECOND CHAMBER

"I am your Jesus, born Incarnate. I have come to further enlighten you as to the Chambers of My Heart. The souls that pass from Holy Love into Divine Love have been convicted in their conscience and purified of their most glaring faults."

"Now as they enter the Second Chamber of My Divine Heart I pour into them knowledge of the virtues, an awareness of the depth of each virtue in their own heart, and a hunger to increase in virtue. For such as these it is not enough just to reach salvation. These souls thirst for holiness, thirst to please Me and draw closer to Me. To them this thirst seems unquenchable. As the virtues deepen they move closer to the next Chamber of My Heart."

"I encharge these Revelations to the world through you. I desire every soul know this call of Holy and Divine Love. It is each soul's response and surrender of his will that appeases My Wounded Heart."

"You will please make all of this known."

January 27, 2001
"THE REVELATION OF OUR UNITED HEARTS"
THE THIRD CHAMBER

"I am your Jesus, born Incarnate. As the soul decides to pursue holiness, he is made more aware of the depth or lack of depth of the virtues in his heart. Every virtue proceeds from love and humility. Therefore, the depth of love and humility in the heart dictates the depth of every virtue."

"Every virtue originates from the power of the Holy Spirit. A person may know how to behave lovingly and humbly, but it is all pretense unless these virtues are alive and thriving in the heart. No virtue originates in the intellect. Further, the one who desires to be known as humble, holy, virtuous is practicing false virtue. The practice of virtue needs to be between the soul and his Creator."

"As the soul attempts to polish the virtues in his heart and refine them in the eyes of God, he enters the Third Chamber of My Heart. In this Chamber the soul finds himself tested over and over in every virtue, for it is the test that strengthens or weakens virtue according to the soul's response."

"This is the Chamber that fine-tunes holiness by testing the virtues as gold in the Flame of Divine Love. As the gold is refined, the soul is prepared for the next Chamber of My Heart."

The Chambers of the United Hearts of Jesus and Mary

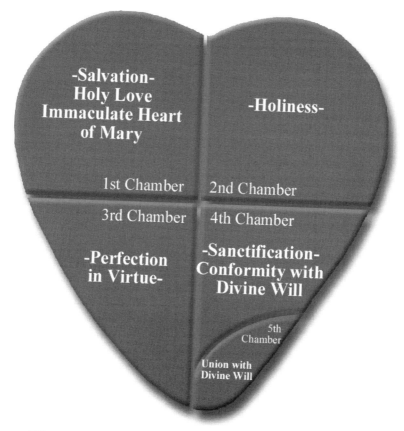

-Salvation-
Holy Love
Immaculate Heart
of Mary

-Holiness-

1st Chamber

2nd Chamber

3rd Chamber

4th Chamber

-Perfection
in Virtue-

-Sanctification-
Conformity with
Divine Will

5th
Chamber

Union with
Divine Will

The Door to Each Chamber is Deeper Surrender to Love — the Divine Will

NOTE: For more information about the Chambers, please see *The Revelation of Our United Hearts: The Secrets Revealed*, published by Archangel Gabriel Enterprises, Inc. and posted in its entirety on the Holy Love website at http://www.holylove.org, along with other publications and messages from Heaven.

August 25, 2000
PRIMER — THE THIRD CHAMBER

"I am your Jesus, born Incarnate. The Third Chamber of My Heart is the one in which My martyrs of love are formed. It is perfection. Thus in the Third Chamber (perfection):

- The soul is given introspection as to his practice of every virtue in thought, word and deed.
- He practices these virtues and fine-tunes them with the help of grace.
- God sees his efforts and infuses the virtues into his soul."

Perfection in the Virtues

March 8, 1999
THE MOUNT TO PERFECTION

"I am here. I am Jesus, born of the flesh. Child, today I will liken the mount to perfection to the construction of a house. The house is made of materials. These are the virtues in the spiritual life. The materials are useless unless the builder puts them together. The builder is your free will. The final product is a thing of beauty to behold, just as a soul is beautiful to Me that seeks union with Me through perfection. The house that is constructed is not only beautiful but can be put to use by many people. This is how I use a soul with many virtues. Such a soul can be used by Me for the good of many others."

June 15, 1999
SURRENDER TO PURIFICATION

"I am your Jesus, born Incarnate. I have come to be reconciled to mankind. The way of reconciliation is the way of Holy Love. When the soul surrenders to the Flame of Holy Love—the Flame of My Mother's Heart, he, in effect, surrenders to purification. I can teach you about every virtue, but with your will you must surrender to them. Holy Love embodies and clothes all the virtues. The more you surrender to Holy Love, the more virtuous you will become. Thus, the deeper you will be in union with Me and the Will of the Father. So you see, your journey in holiness depends on you. Your surrender to Divine and Holy Love is a freedom. Your heart is not tethered by affairs of the world. All of these you give to Me in Holy Trust."

January 15, 2001
VIRTUES ARE POWER TOOLS

"I am your Jesus, born Incarnate. Today I have come to help you understand why Holy Love is the path of salvation. No one enters My

Father's kingdom who does not love God above all else and his neighbor as himself."

"My messages to you concerning the Chambers of My Heart are as a blueprint to heaven, holiness and sanctity. There are many who do not know this path or my plan. For them, salvation is more complicated, holiness elusive, and sanctity an unrealistic goal. It is as though they are trying to build a house without a blueprint. Besides this, they have no power tools. These power tools I give you are the virtues."

"So you see, through this Message I have drawn for each soul a blueprint and am willing to give him power tools, as well, to construct his own house or heart of Holy Love. The more closely he follows My plan, the more perfect his house will be."

"Some are master carpenters, others not so willing to learn. But I am a patient teacher—a merciful taskmaster. And so, you will please make this known."

October 30, 2000
HOLY PERFECTION VS. PERFECTIONISM

"I am your Jesus, born Incarnate. I have come to discuss with you the difference between holy perfection and being a perfectionist. The one who seeks to be perfected in the virtues does so out of love of Me. The one who seeks perfectionism in the worldly sense has created a barrier between My Heart and his own."

"To desire holiness and perfection in the virtues is a lofty goal provided the only concern is to please God. Such a one does not concern himself for worldly esteem. He is at peace—cooperating with the Divine Will of My Father."

"The worldly perfectionist is greatly concerned with the way others perceive him. If he should make a mistake, he is quick to make excuses and blame others. It is difficult for such a one to acknowledge his own error. The perfectionist is not content with looking into his own heart, but he can readily see the errors of all those around him."

"While the one who tries to be perfected in virtue loses his own will in the Will of God—the perfectionist is full of opinions which he cannot let go of readily. The perfectionist most often has himself at the center of his thoughts and motives, while the one who seeks perfection in the virtues tries to always have love of God at the center of his thoughts, words and actions."

"The perfectionist has trouble forgiving both himself and others. But Holy Love always makes allowances. In humility the soul must forgive and understand that human forgiveness is a mirror of the soul's humility and a shadow of God's infinite Mercy."

"Make it known."

December 28, 2000
THE PATH OF SPIRITUAL CLEANSING

"I am your Jesus, born Incarnate. My messenger, to you and through you I have opened the door to the innermost Chambers of My Heart. You must know and help others to comprehend that the only way to progress through these Chambers is through a deepening awareness of self—that is becoming aware of the flavor within your own soul contrary to Holy and Divine Love. This takes honesty and courage. If a person cannot accept that he has an area in his heart that is not perfected in love, then he cannot repair the error either."

"Recently, My Mother told you to take the many chores you needed to do around the house little by little. After the holidays and your illness, they had piled up. She said do not attempt to get them done in one day, but to take several days and accomplish a little at a time. It is the same with a spiritual housecleaning. The areas of pride in your soul need to be overcome little by little. It is easy to feel overwhelmed if you look at all the spiritual cleansing your soul needs. But you are not cleaning the household of your soul alone. I will help you. No one becomes humble or forgiving in thought only and is genuinely humble—forgiving."

"I have to work in the heart for true humility to take root. But just as the soul cannot accomplish this virtue alone, I cannot put humility in the heart without the soul's assistance. The soul with courage has to admit where his house needs to be cleaned, where is pride winning out. Then he and I can together conquer the pride."

"So many are unwilling to even look for the dusty areas of their heart. It is a painful discovery to some to first realize their own imperfections. But I will sustain them if they would only be humble enough to ask. Even with My assistance, they need courage to recognize and overcome Satan who tries to convince them they are fine as is."

"So I have come to ask you to pray for those who desire to advance into My Heart but refuse the path of spiritual cleansing."

January 10, 2000
THE PURSUIT OF SANCTITY

"I am your Jesus, born Incarnate. I have come to encourage you. Let us compare the spiritual journey with that of an athlete. An athlete takes many steps before he is hailed as a champion. He may make many sacrifices and endure vigorous training until one day all things work together bringing him to his best effort. Now he always remembers the taste of victory and makes it his goal and his pursuit from then on."

"The soul too, who endeavors towards sanctity, must put forth much effort and make numerous sacrifices. He must practice virtue and endure many tests. If he perseveres, the soul, like the athlete, is victorious. In that special moment when human effort and Heavenly grace come together, the soul is transported to the fourth...Chamber of My Heart. His trophy is not cast of metal, but is sweet union with his God. He may not remain long in this Chamber but, like the athlete who tastes victory, the soul longs for this union with every breath. He may become weak in one area of his spiritual life and have to re-shape his heart over and over, just as an athlete must maintain a strong body."

"But the sweetness of the soul's victory—no matter how brief—lingers with him. Like a favored melody, the memory of this most intimate Chamber drifts back into the soul over and over calling to him. Do not be discouraged if your every effort is not worthy of this Fourth Chamber. Your whole life is a spiritual journey. Unlike the athlete, age is not your enemy. Every present moment is a new opportunity to win sanctity."

"You will please make this known."

May 12, 2006
PRACTICE STRENGTHENS VIRTUE
"I am your Jesus, born Incarnate."

"Today I have come to help you understand that to increase in any virtue, the soul must practice the virtue. Say, for instance, the soul needs to increase in patience. This is a very common deficit in modern society, as instant gratification is encouraged. In order to gain strength in the virtue of patience, the soul must not give in to impatience, for to do so weakens the virtue and strengthens the flaw."

"It is so with every virtue. If a soul needs to trust more, I will give him many opportunities to trust Me so that he can increase in this virtue. It is always evil that tempts the soul away from virtue and into weakness. So you see, it is with free will the soul moves away from human weakness and becomes stronger in virtue—the building blocks of holiness."

January 12, 2002
SAINTS PRACTICE HEROIC VIRTUE
"I am your Jesus, born Incarnate. I have come to explain to you the difference between holiness and sanctity. The holy one is righteous in many ways. He tries to lead a virtuous life most of the time. When he remembers to keep Me in the center of his heart he practices Holy Love. But there are, nevertheless, small areas of his heart he does not surrender to Me. Perhaps he does not consider the source of inspirations that come to him and, therefore, speaks or acts uncharitably. Perhaps through inordinate self-love, he is attached to the world in some way—be it his reputation, his opinion or his appearance."

"Now the soul who reaches sanctity leaves everything behind except his love for Me and for his neighbor. The difference between the one who is holy and the one who is saintly is that the saint practices heroic virtue. Heroic virtue is virtue that the soul perseveres in <u>despite personal cost</u>. Therefore, when he is patient he has no thought towards 'poor me—I must be patient in the face of this annoyance'. He does not consider himself humble or holy, but regards all others as more virtuous than himself and constantly pursues a deeper perfection in virtue. He is always ready to 'go the extra mile' for Me."

"You will please make this known."

March 10, 2003
HEROIC VIRTUE AMIDST TRIALS

"I am your Jesus, born Incarnate. In every present moment the soul is given the grace to be heroic in virtue. All that stops him is his free will. He hesitates—considering the cost to himself. In the instant that he hesitates, Satan is present urging him to act contrary to virtue. If the soul is being tested in patience and meekness, Satan tempts him with thoughts of anger. If the test is in humility, the devil invokes thoughts of self-love and pride. But the soul can only advance in perfection of the virtue when he practices the virtue amidst trials—<u>for it is in the test that the virtue comes to perfection.</u>"

"The soul must never consider himself perfect in any virtue. He should never think: 'I was patient yesterday so now I have perfected the virtue of patience'—for the next test may be even greater than the last. Each soul needs to ask for the grace upon arising to be virtuous throughout the day."

"Say upon arising:"

"Dear Jesus, through the Immaculate Heart of Mary, open my heart to the grace I need to be perfected in virtue today in every present moment. Amen."

November 12, 2001
TESTS OF VIRTUE

Jesus and Blessed Mother are here with Their Hearts exposed. Blessed Mother says: "Praise be to Jesus."

Jesus: "I am your Jesus, born Incarnate. My brothers and sisters, I have come tonight to help you understand that you cannot be courageous unless your courage is tested; nor can you trust, unless you are tested in trust. Remember, it is in the test that every virtue comes to perfection."

"Tonight We are blessing you with the Blessing of Our United Hearts."

December 1, 2001
TEMPTATIONS

St. Thomas Aquinas comes. He is walking down the aisle with great difficulty due to his weight. He says: "Praise be to Jesus. Daughter, tell Fr. Kenney that I appear in this bodily form so that you will recognize me when you compare my vision to photographs in the past. After all, ask him to recall that Moses and Elijah appeared in bodily form at the Transfiguration, but they are not body and soul in Heaven, as yet."

"I have come to speak to you today about temptation. Temptation is the test of virtue. Without the test—without temptation—the soul cannot practice virtue, and cannot be perfected in the virtue being tested. Therefore, temptation can bring good or evil according to the soul's response."

"Do not be surprised, then, when I tell you that the Message of Holy Love brings out the best and the worst in people. It brings out the best when the soul recognizes his faults through immersion in the Flame of Holy Love, and tries to overcome his faults—that is, be perfected in virtue. The Message brings out the worst in the soul when his faults are revealed to him, but he makes little or no effort to overcome them."

"So, it is the choice each soul makes in the face of temptation that determines the depth of his journey into the Chambers of the United Hearts. It is the depth of love in the heart that determines the response to each temptation."

"Let me explain: If you have great love of God and neighbor in your heart (Holy Love), you will want, at all cost, to avoid hurting God and neighbor. Therefore, supposing you are tempted to be impatient, you will, in the face of temptation, practice patience. See then, it is God's Permitting Will that allows temptation to come into each one's life, for He desires that you be strong in virtue."

"I must return to Heaven now, but you will please make this known."

March 21, 2005
CROSSES

Jesus and Blessed Mother are here with Their Hearts exposed. Blessed Mother says: "Praise be to Jesus."

Jesus: "I am your Jesus, born Incarnate. Tonight I want to give you new meaning to the Cross. See the vertical beam as a channel of God's Will for you. See the crossbeam as your embrace of God's Will. Every cross is a test in one or more of the virtues. Therefore, understand that every cross comes to you as My call to come into Divine Union."

"Tonight We're blessing you with the Blessing of Our United Hearts."

September 3, 2001
SURRENDER TO THE CROSS

Jesus and Blessed Mother are here with Their Hearts exposed. Blessed Mother says: "Praise be to Jesus."

Jesus: "I am your Jesus, born Incarnate. My brothers and sisters, in order for the cross to be meritorious, it needs to be surrendered to, and given back to Me as a gift. Then the soul will receive an eternal reward greater than if he had not submitted to his cross."

"In order for the soul to surrender to a cross, many virtues must be present in his heart first—love, humility, patience, and meekness, to name a few. If you pray and ask for the grace to accept and surrender to your crosses, Heaven will assist you."

"We're extending to you tonight the Blessing of Our United Hearts."

Obstacles to Holiness

March 24, 2000
MOST COMMON OBSTACLES

"I am your Jesus, born Incarnate. I have come to lay bare the obstacles most common to the soul who first decides to choose Holy Love. Sometimes these are obstacles that remain with the soul all along his spiritual journey, as the soul does not recognize them."

"The first is unforgiveness, which bears the evil fruit of a bitter heart. Thus when you first choose holiness you must forgive everyone. If you do not, the virtuous life will elude you."

"The next obstacle is that of judging others. This is an open entrapment of Satan and stems from self-righteousness—a form of spiritual pride. This error has a sister, which is spiritual envy. A soul should never compare his spiritual progress to another."

"Yet another obstacle to the spiritual journey is discouragement. When the soul's faults are revealed to him, instead of overcoming them in the present moment, he may be tempted to live in the past or the future. But sorrow for sin belongs in the present where the soul understands the fullness of My Mercy. Therefore, in the present the soul trusts that My Mercy over his past removes his guilt forever."

"Understand that Satan does not want your holiness. He is eager for the soul to choose any obstacle through self-will. Be aware of his actions and pitfalls. Discover them and avoid them."

"I will bless you."

August 17, 2006
FAULTS

St. Martin de Porres says: "Praise be to Jesus."

"All of the faults which present themselves as obstacles to deeper holiness, such as unforgiveness, anger, self-centeredness, jealousy—these are all signs of weakness in Holy Love. These Messages are meant to root out such flaws and make room in the heart for a more profound quality of Holy Love. This is why each soul needs to look with courage and humility into his own heart each day, and throughout the day to see if he is making the right choices in every present moment. To live otherwise is only carelessness."

May 1, 1999
LESSON ON ATTACHMENTS

"It is I, Jesus, the Word born Incarnate. Child, I have come to help you understand the mutual love I call you to. The law of Holy Love is to love the Lord thy God with your whole heart, soul, and mind, and your neighbor as yourself. This is the way to union with the Divine Will, the way to holiness, sanctity. Anything, person or place, that obstructs the way, represents an attachment."

"So today, I would like to teach you about attachments. It is Satan who tries to carry your heart away. He suggests you should be worried about your appearance, your reputation, where you live, or what you are to eat. He keeps your heart in turmoil through unforgiveness. He suggests you must not give up your own opinion, which is the trap of self-righteousness. Within this same attachment to opinion lies another snare, that of judging. All of these fill your heart with thoughts contrary to love of God and neighbor."

"When you come before Me to pray, anything that your mind clings to in the natural is some sort of attachment. If you love Me with your whole heart it is easy to surrender everything to Me. It is easy to trust Me. But you do not trust Me if you cannot see My grace at work in every aspect of your life through My Love for you."

"Attachments are Satan's tool, his way of pulling you away from Me. If you ask Me I will help you overcome every barrier, but you must want it. Come to Me completely. Free yourselves of all that stands between us. I will bless you."

May 8, 1999
ATTACHMENTS

"I am your Jesus, born Incarnate. I invite you to contemplate for a moment a balloon on a string. The string is tied to something and holding the balloon down. Such is the human will when it holds some attachment in its heart. When the string is cut, the little balloon soars into the heavens and disappears. So I desire the human heart to be detached from all things, people, or places that hold it down. When the soul accomplishes this and breaks its tethers, it soars to Heaven; the human will disappears and the soul is united to the Divine Will of God."

"Why do I come through time and space to tell you this? Because being one with the Divine Will is the height, the breadth, and the depth of holiness. It is union with My Divine Love—My Sacred Heart. The time will come in each soul when it is stripped and standing before Me. I will judge each one according to how much they loved—not the world—but God and neighbor. At that precise moment, popularity, appearance, wealth, and power will amount to nothing."

"The Divine Will of God is Holy Love in the present moment. It is your refuge and salvation. Choose it. I choose it for you."

March 23, 2007
FALSE VIRTUE

Jesus is here with His Heart exposed. He says: "I am your Jesus, born Incarnate."

"My brothers and sisters, with a loving Heart I come tonight to warn you of a particular pitfall along the spiritual journey—that of false virtue. False virtue is practiced for others to see. False spirituality claims gifts that are not really present in the soul; take for instance, false discernment which leads people to believe Satan's lies. Pray for the strength to be humble of heart and you will avoid these pitfalls."

"Tonight I'm blessing you with My Blessing of Divine Love."

Prayer Life

April 24, 1999
LESSON ON PRAYER

"I have come to you today as your Jesus, born Incarnate. I wish today to teach you about prayer. Prayer is a refuge or weapon and a means of unification—creature to Creator. The more the soul surrenders his own will to the Will of God, the deeper his union through prayer."

"Surrender then your plans, your choices, your desires. No good comes to you except through God. In this surrender you are engaging all the virtues—faith, hope, love, humility, simplicity, meekness, trust."

"Prayer is communication with God, either in the heart, on the lips, or through any action that is surrendered to the Divine Will."

"My Mother prays with you when you pray the Rosary. Her Heart is a channel through which your prayers ascend to Heaven and grace passes back down to you. Her Heart is a connection then to God and God's grace, just as you would connect an electric light to currents."

"God receives the sacrifice of prayer and uses it as a sword against evil. He changes the prayer into grace that overcomes evil in hearts. Then see, it is Satan that tries to keep you from praying. It is Satan who embattles your heart and tries to keep you from surrendering your will so that you can pray."

"No matter your course of action in any event, everything depends on God. Trust this. The soul that trusts only in himself is lost."

"Think of prayer as a sunbeam. Its ray stretches down from Heaven. It nourishes the lilies and flowers. It royally clothes them in light. Thus arrayed, they bloom and their beauty gives glory to God. The soul that surrenders to prayer much, also becomes beautiful in God's eyes and gives glory to God."

"I have told you, My confidante, that prayer is a surrender and a sacrifice. But the soul must also accept the way prayers are answered. The little flower receives what it needs to be nourished and grow. The soul, through prayer, receives what it needs for salvation. In humility, he must accept God's Will. If the Father knows what the little flower needs, does he not know your needs as well? Accept what He sends you in humility and gratefulness, like the little flower dancing in the sunlight."

"I am pleased with any prayer. Most of all I am pleased with sincere prayer from the heart. This kind of prayer changes people and events. I, your Jesus, love the prayer of the Mass the most. Then I love the Rosary."

"Follow Me in prayer. I will lead you."

April 27, 1999
VIRTUE OF PRAYER

"I am your Jesus, born Incarnate. Come into My Divine Love. Today, I have come to help you understand the virtue of prayer. Just as the sunbeam shines down from Heaven and invites the flower to open and bloom, so every inspiration to pray is an invitation—a call— from My Divine Love to prayer. So often My invitations go unanswered, for Satan opposes prayer more than any other good. Look at the world around you. Everywhere that prayer has been discouraged, evil has taken over. In families the adversary has been able to divide, for few families pray <u>together</u>. In schools where prayer was banned, you now have drugs and violence. In government bodies instead of prayer you have legalized abortion. Even here in this Mission where prayer is the mainstay, you are feared by some and others look askance at you. The ones who come often and support the prayer effort should be commended for their perseverance and fortitude."

"Every prayer makes a difference in the world and in the balance between good and evil. The prayer that rises out of a heart full of Holy Love is most worthy. This type of prayer unites, converts, changes people and events, sanctifies and makes whole."

"A life of prayer is indeed itself a mission. It is a call from Divine Love."

May 27, 1999
POWER OF PRAYER

When I [Maureen] arrived at the chapel, Jesus was there with His Heart exposed. He motioned for me to sit down. He said: "Today, I will speak to you. I am Jesus, born Incarnate. My Sovereignty is over every heart. Now the world realizes how Satan has been working in hearts to gain his end. There is no more arms race. All are equal. For while people did not realize prayer was the answer and the rosary was the

Mary, Refuge of Holy Love

weapon of choice, Satan stealthily gained control of countries unwilling to accept Christian standards. Every place you go, everywhere you speak, you must stress the power of prayer. Encourage My people to pray even if only a little."

"The way to peace is through the Heart of My Mother. Her Immaculate Heart is Holy Love. People may think they are coming directly to Me in prayer, and think they have the advantage over less 'enlightened' souls. I tell you the truth: just as no one comes to the Father except through Me, no one comes to Me except through the Heart of My Mother. The grace of Her Heart invites people to prayer. Because My Mother's Heart is Holy Love and Holy Love is the Will of God, there is no passage to Me around the Immaculate Heart. Everyone that prays to Me does so by My Mother's invitation. No one prays who does not love to some degree."

"For these reasons, My call to humanity is Holy Love, Holy Love, Holy Love. It is this call that will defeat Satan who seeks to destroy the world and gain every soul for himself. Do not allow him to achieve this. Pray, pray, pray."

Lessons
on
The Virtues

Holy and Divine Love

January 12, 1999
LESSON ON LOVE

Jesus comes, His arms outstretched. He says: "I am Jesus, born Incarnate. Come into My Heart of Divine Love. There is but one door. It is Holy Love. I come to you to teach you the way. Follow the path I now lay bare before you, lest you trip and fall. This lesson is on love. I will teach you the way of every virtue. Holy Love embraces every virtue. It is the embodiment of all commandments. It is the mecca of holiness. If Holy Love could be seen, it would be sunlight enlightening good and revealing evil. If it could be felt, it would be the embrace of Heaven. If it could be tasted, it would be the foretaste of the New Jerusalem."

"Holy Love is everything—the sum total—the surrender to salvation."

"No one enters My Father's Kingdom who does not love Him with heart, mind, and soul. No one enters who does not love his neighbor as much as himself."

"This is how you love: you decide to do it. Without the surrender of your will, it is not possible to live in Love. How sweet your surrender! How sweet! It is only and always in the present moment I seek it."

"It is the way to Divine Love."

January 11, 1999
SURRENDER TO LOVE

Jesus appears with a little lamb in His arms. He says: "I am Jesus, born of the Flesh. I have come to let all people know the depth of My Divine Love. I pour out My Love on all people—all nations. Some hearts, please understand, reject Me. Remember the ice that lay over the snow up north? You walked on it, but did not sink through it to the snow. Do you recall, little heart?"

"Yes."

"Such is a heart that will not surrender to love. I cannot reach it, as it is encased in its own will. Let Me explain the merits of surrendering to Love, for I am Love."

"Through surrender, you give all to My Mother—interior and exterior. She, in turn, gives it to Me. Then, I am able to come into your heart. This is called Holy Possession. You give to My Mother everything:"

"You surrender your reputation. Then Satan cannot attack you through people's opinions. (Hmmm…. People's opinions. Some act as though it's their most prized possession. They can't take it with them.)"

"You surrender the Mission and its course, which stands protected and provided for through Divine grace."

"You surrender your appearance. I look at your heart."

"You surrender your health and well-being. I will give you what you need."

"You surrender all your spiritual gifts and worldly possessions, making them Mine."

"Now, as St. Paul says, over all these things put on love. Holy and Divine Love will fill—and fill to overflowing—anything you empty yourself of. You will not need to seek happiness anywhere in the world. You will be happy."

"This is how Divine Love comes into the soul and works, little heart. It takes dying to self and loving Me, as My Mother has been teaching you."

"I am leaving you now so that you can assimilate all I have said, and make it known."

January 12, 2004
DIVINE LOVE

St. Thomas Aquinas says: "Praise be to Jesus."

"I have come to give you deeper understanding of Divine Love. The Heart of Jesus is Love and Mercy. These two cannot exist in any heart apart from one another. As every virtue is perfect in the Sacred Heart of Jesus, Divine Love and Divine Mercy are perfect in His Divine Heart. But there are other virtues and attributes which are also perfect in His Heart, and they are woven into Love and Mercy, making up the very fiber of Love and Mercy. Two of these are Justice and Truth. These depend on each other and on Love and Mercy for their very existence."

"Love lays the foundation for Mercy. Mercy is interwoven with Justice and Truth. These are all threads that comprise the Sacred Heart. The more the soul surrenders to Divine Love, the more closely he imitates these attributes, and the more tightly woven is the fabric of his own heart."

"Every attribute of the Sacred Heart interacts with all the other Holy and Divine attributes. This is the goal of personal holiness, for when one attribute or virtue is weak, the 'thread' is pulled loose and the soul runs the risk of unraveling his entire tapestry of holiness."

March 30, 1999
THE CALL TO HOLY AND DIVINE LOVE

Jesus comes in white with much light around Him and around His Heart. He says: "I am your Jesus, born Incarnate. How can I describe to you the confines of My Heart? The soul that lives in My Divine Love understands that I have always loved him and always will love him. He understands that every cross is a victory if it is surrendered to Me. In that surrender is the merit for every soul. The deeper the surrender, the greater the merit. The soul in union with Me in Divine Love knows that nothing holds value except holiness and salvation. Anything in the way, any obstacle that the soul stops at, is either through his free will or a temptation from Satan."

"The depths of My Heart are complete peace. It is in the quiet of your soul you have felt this—in the far distant train whistle during the night—in the song bird as you awaken on a spring morning—in the crickets hymn as night falls in the spring. All of these are glimpses of the New Jerusalem and union with My Divine Love."

"My Mother comes to you on the sweet breeze of Heaven—the fragrance of roses. She wants you to understand that it is Her grace and your efforts that will lead you deeper into virtue, just as the fragrance of a rose draws you closer to the flower."

"Self-love accomplishes the opposite. It pulls you away from Me. It is what you want towards esteem in the world or comfort and consolation. Attempts at holiness are always rendered fruitful through grace when they are sincere. This is once again a 'simple' call, but difficult in the eyes of the world."

April 7, 1999
HOLY AND DIVINE LOVE

Jesus comes in white. He says, "I am your Jesus, born Incarnate. Alleluia! Today, My child, I have come to help you understand that the greatest achievement, no matter its value to humanity, is not as great as the least effort in Holy Love. For Holy Love pleases Me and is directed towards pleasing Me. There is no self-interest in this call. It is the response I have come to seek."

"Divine Love is like whipped cream on a dessert." He smiles so much I see His teeth. He knows I love whipped cream. "It makes the soul see how palatable every act of Holy Love is—how pleasing each act is to Me. Or it is like the sandal worn thin walking many places doing much for his brethren, but made more comfortable through its miles of wear than any new sandal. Divine Love becomes compatible with Holy Love in the soul without great fanfare, but through perseverance in holiness by way of Holy Love."

"It is then the soul is united to Me—becomes inseparable from Me—chooses Me. My Heart is the repose of the holy, the Flame that longs to engulf humanity. There is only one way to attain the treasure of this union. It is through Holy Love."

July 7, 2003
HOLY LOVE VS. WORLDLY LOVE

"I am your Jesus, born Incarnate—Divine Love, Divine Mercy. I have come to help you understand the difference between love as the world knows it and Holy Love which leads to Heaven."

"Worldly love is an emotion—an affection—for a particular person, situation or thing. It does not lead beyond the temporary veil of this world. It is often self-seeking and sensual."

"Holy Love, on the other hand, is an affection of the spirit. This type of love calls the soul deep into personal holiness, virtue and Heaven itself. Holy Love brings the affections of the heart into union with the affections of the soul. When free will is finally given over to Holy Love—love of God above all else and neighbor as self—the soul begins his conformity to the Divine Will of My Father."

"In final judgment I look at the degree of Holy Love that has governed the soul's free will throughout his life, and especially as he drew his last breath."

September 24, 1999
HOLY LOVE EMBRACES EVERY VIRTUE

"I am your Jesus, born Incarnate. Today I have come seeking your greater understanding of the virtues. The Holy Love in your heart in the present moment forms the vessel that embraces every virtue. The vessel is strengthened by surrender to Holy Love and weakened by self-love. Because Holy Love is the vessel that embraces every other virtue, know and understand that the depth of all virtue and the value of every act is determined by the degree of surrender to Holy Love."

"I am calling you to understand this and by virtue of the Message of Holy Love make it known."

July 9, 1999
SURRENDER TO HOLY LOVE

"Understand as I speak to you that I am Jesus, the Word born Incarnate. My Eucharistic Heart is the center of the universe. But this Heart cannot save a single soul unless the soul surrenders to Holy Love. The degree of surrender determines the degree of sanctity. Indeed, self-abandonment is the key to salvation."

"Souls cannot love Me or trust Me or even know Me who allow their hearts to be full of themselves. Self-love is always the door Satan walks through. Self-love is inordinate love of power, money, ambition, reputation, sensuality, greed—all these that are from Satan."

"But when the soul surrenders to Holy Love, he is willing to give up everything, all his own 'wants', for Me."

"Such a soul has no need for recognition. Such a one despises the limelight and has no concern for reputation. He does not promote himself or his own agenda, but waits in the background to quietly do My bidding. If he accomplishes something on My behalf, He does not look for credit, but gives thanks to God. These humble souls that surrender to Holy Love are the instruments I delight to use. These are the ones that allow Holy Love to take over their hearts. They place all My needs ahead of their own."

"These are the ones I call My own."

November 26, 2000 - Conversation with Divine Love
HOLY LOVE IS LIKE A SYMPHONY

"I am your Jesus, born Incarnate. Child, understand that Holy Love is much like a symphony. A symphony requires the performance of many instruments to make up the whole. In Holy Love, the soul must try to perfect himself in many virtues in order to come into the bosom of the virtue of Holy Love."

"I have asked of you martyrdom—to be a martyr of love—and this is what martyrdom is: complete dying to self for love of God. You cannot achieve this on your own merit, but only with My help. It is selfish love that detracts from every virtue. Do not be distraught when I try to show you the areas of self-love in your heart, for I desire your purest effort. It is then I can succeed through you. Remember, you have not chosen this mission on your own. Rather, I have called you and you have responded. You ask how I desire that your response be more complete. I am showing you. Do not back away in discouragement as I reveal areas of weakness in your heart, but move forward with Me. I will help you overcome each flaw, for your perfection is in Me and through Me—just as this mission is in Me and through Me."

"Great is My Love for those who allow Me to assist them! Great is My joy!"

November 27, 2000
SYMPHONY OF SURRENDER

"I am your Jesus, born Incarnate, Lord of Mercy and Love. I have come to help you understand that a symphony is only sweet when each instrument is played to perfection. So too, Holy Love in the heart does not reach its fullness until the virtues are practiced in their perfection. The human heart is incapable of perfect love or perfect virtue by his own efforts, but it is capable of purifying its efforts in the virtues through My grace."

"Therefore, the orchestration of the heart's efforts in holiness are in harmony with perfection (which is God's Will) when he cooperates with grace which leads him to be more and more perfect. Such efforts rise to Heaven as a sweet symphony of surrender. It is chanted throughout Heaven by all the angels. Then it rises to the nostrils of the Eternal Father as a fragrant incense. So sweet to Heaven are the soul's efforts in holiness through grace. Make it known."

February 27, 2002 - Conversation with Divine Love
HOW TO LIVE IN HOLY LOVE

Jesus comes walking towards me on what appears to be water. He says: "Let this image always conjure sentiments of trust in Me. I am your Jesus, born Incarnate."

"Today I have come to describe to you how to live in Holy Love. Make yourself very little in My Heart. Forget about yourself. Do not worry about how others regard you, but only concern yourself with pleasing Me in every present moment. So often sins are committed in thought, word and deed out of concern for the opinions of others. Put Me always at the center of your heart so that I am in your every thought, word and deed."

"Respect the poor. Have compassion for the downhearted. Lead the spiritually impoverished. Your greatest efforts to assist others are made greater through your love and trust in Me. It is only by grace you can accomplish any good. It is only in littleness your love of Me comes to perfection."

March 31, 2004
AGAPE LOVE

"I am your Jesus, born Incarnate. At the heart of this Message is selfless love. This is agape love—a love that has no hidden agenda towards selfish motives. This is love in its purest form. With what eagerness do I answer prayers that come to Me rising from a heart full of such pure love! It is this type of love that embraced the Cross and redeemed mankind. It is this kind of love that comes to this site and calls souls to conversion and into the Chambers of Divine Love. This is the love that with purity of intention brings souls into the very depths of union with the Divine Will."

The Pharisees acted out of self-love and condemned Me out of fear. The same holds true today as your persecutors conceal hidden agendas in their hearts. Pray for those who persecute you. Such a prayer surrendered to Me with pure love will win many graces for this Mission—more than you can comprehend."

April 29, 1998
SELF-LOVE VS. HOLY LOVE

"Ah! At last we are alone, and I can confide in you."

"The path of holiness—the path of Holy Love—can only be followed through self-abasement. By forgetting self and how all things affect self, the soul can love Me, come to Me, abide in Me."

"It is so, that I am able to lead and guide each soul deep into My

Mother's heart—then into My Own Heart. Think about Me and My needs instead of your own. When you forget about yourself, you are able to trust Me. When you focus on your own problems, you call them back into your heart instead of surrendering them to Me. Loving Me makes you strong. Loving yourself makes you weak. Respect yourself as God's creation, but focus on Me. I will take care of you. I will lead you. I will not forsake you. You can trust Me."

"When a soul is thus able to die to self, he is in My embrace. When His life is Christ-centered, he has joy and peace. Thus, will you find weaknesses and faults vanish."

"Abide in Me. Abide in Me. Forget self. Abide in Me."

SELF-LOVE	HOLY-LOVE
Christ is pushed out of the center of our lives, and self is made the center.	God and others are made center of lives.
Hangs on to every wrong perpetrated against him.	Forgives.
Considers himself holy, worthy of consolations and grace.	Knows he can always be more holy. Knows all spiritual gifts are not his but God's, and he is unworthy of them. God disposes favors as He chooses.
Trusts only human efforts. Cannot let go and let God. Hangs on to problems by focusing on them. Won't allow grace to take over.	Surrenders all things to God's grace. Trusts God to bring good to every situation.

April 10, 1999
SELF-LOVE VS. HOLY LOVE

Jesus stands in front of me in red and white. "I am your Jesus, born Incarnate. I have come to you today to help you understand the effects of self-love. Once again, self-love is an inordinate self-centeredness that takes you away from love of God and neighbor. The soul opens himself to trusting only things in the world (money - power) and is led away from trusting in Me. I have given mankind the world to use towards his own salvation and holiness. In this way, he uses the world and its attributes to give glory to God and to express love towards his neighbor."

"It is this self-love that contributes greatly to false virtues. A false virtue is one that is practiced for show—to impress others—or to gain merit for self in the eyes of others. Anyone who tries to act loving, humble, or meek to impress others is guilty of this false virtue. The virtues are given to build up your own personal holiness within your own heart. This should be accomplished in simplicity and in the secret recesses of your heart. Your journey in holiness should be between you and Me, not for others to see."

"When you are judged it will be just you and Me. No one else's opinion will matter. You will be unable to offer excuses for what I see in your heart."

"This is how you should live then—with your eyes fixed on Heaven and your hearts steeped in Holy Love. I give each one no other call."

November 11, 2002
SELF-LOVE VS. HOLY LOVE

St. Thomas Aquinas comes. He says: "Praise be to Jesus."

"I have come to help each one see that the true enemy is that which opposes Holy Love in the heart. It is always insidious—even clothed in righteousness at times. But the culprit is always self-interest, self-love—above and ahead of God and neighbor. It may come into the heart as negative criticism of others—soon spawning unforgiveness—then bitterness. Self-love invites the soul to criticize others thus holding himself up in higher esteem. It may be love of material goods, sensuality or even love of his own opinion that drives Holy Love from the heart."

"But where the cancer that consumes Holy Love begins is always inordinate self-love. This is why the conversion process always begins with loving God more than self. It is this love that opens the heart to the Flame of Holy Love."

June 27, 2005
HOLY LOVE MIRRORS THE SOUL

St. Thomas Aquinas says: "Praise be to Jesus."

"I have come to help you understand that Holy Love is the mirror which reflects the state of your soul. In this mirror the depth of Holy Love in your heart is reflected along with the reflection of all other virtues—for love is the light that shines through all virtues. It is self-love that clouds this mirror and does not allow the soul to see clearly the depth of virtue in his heart or his errors and faults."

"Holy Love is the mirror all souls need to gaze into to see their inner beauty which reveals how they appear in God's Eyes. This is the appearance and beauty that needs careful attendance—continual attendance."

"The depth of every virtue in the soul is reflected in the depth of Holy Love in the heart; for instance, the soul can only be as patient as he is loving. He can only be as humble as he is loving. To pretend otherwise is false virtue, and not a reflection of Holy Love."

"This is why the soul must continually weigh and measure his thoughts, words and deeds on the scale of Holy Love. Only then will he be a more perfect image of Holy Love for all to behold."

August 21, 2006
DEPTH OF HOLY LOVE

St. Thomas Aquinas says: "Praise be to Jesus."

"Today I have come to help you understand that the depth of Holy Love in your heart determines the depth of every virtue, as well. Knowing this truth, you must realize that you should pray daily to come deeper into Holy and Divine Love. It is through love of God and love of neighbor that you receive a more generous nature, making you bear others' faults patiently, overcoming jealousy and unforgiveness; indeed, increasing in every virtue so as to steady your feet upon the path of perfection."

"So then, realize that Holy Love is like a fountain of life—overflowing into each heart that welcomes it. However, no one can draw near this fountain unless he first embraces Holy and Divine Love."

January 18, 2006
SECRET OF PERFECTION IN HOLY AND DIVINE LOVE

St. Thomas Aquinas comes. He says: "Praise be to Jesus."

"I have come to help each one understand that true perfection in Holy Love and Divine Love only comes from God. The most the soul can do is to predispose his heart towards perfection by struggling with his free will to keep love of God and neighbor in the center of his heart."

"Satan attacks this predisposition through self-love—attraction to the allurements of the world—love of money, power and reputation. Perfect love of God and neighbor withers and dies in such an environment. It must remain a constant struggle of the free will to keep God's Law of Love in the center of the heart. This is the secret of perfection."

Humility, Simplicity and Love

November 28, 1998
HOLY HUMILITY AND HOLY LOVE

Jesus: "If humility is the root of every virtue, understand that Holy Love is the soil in which it grows. The tree that bears all virtue cannot thrive without roots and soil."

"Every virtue is practiced by a movement of free will. It is infused into the soul through the persevering practice of the virtue."

"First, the soul must choose Holy Love—the soil. Through love of God above all else and love of neighbor as self, the soul must practice humility."

"Humility is self-abasing, thus open to self-knowledge—even welcomes it. Humility then sees criticism as a grace, considers others more worthy of grace, esteem, reward than himself. Humility is happy with the lowliest job, and never seeks recognition for his efforts. Humility seeks to be hidden. Thus a person who claims humility is far from it."

"In Paul to Corinthians, Chapter 13, Paul describes Holy Love. This is also a description of Holy Humility."

January 13, 1999
LESSON ON HOLY HUMILITY

Jesus comes. Many lights (angels) precede Him. "I have come to give glory to the Father. I am Jesus Incarnate. Child, are you ready for today's lesson?"

Maureen: "Yes."

Jesus: "Today I will teach you about Holy Humility, as humility and love go hand in hand. A soul cannot progress along the path to the Kingdom of Divine Love outside of either of these two. The humble soul has died to his self-will. He has surrendered all to Me, and I to the Father. The humble one is like a little child who takes direction easily, and entrusts all aspects of his well-being to his parents."

"It is the humble who progress rapidly in the spiritual life, bringing many souls to Me. He succeeds in this by performing unpleasant tasks without complaint and in hiddenness. The truly humble is repelled by compliments, positions of importance, or power. Insults are of no consequence to the humble. Reputation has been surrendered to Me. The humble one does not take pride in his opinion, spirituality, or any attribute God has granted him."

"How does one achieve humility? Guard against the enemy of humility which is pride. It was pride that told Satan to say, 'I will not serve.' Practice humility of heart in pride's place. I will help you, if you ask."

"It is I who call you into the Kingdom of My Heart."

February 21, 2007
LOVE OF HUMILITY

St. Martin de Porres says: "Praise be to Jesus."

"Today I have come to invite you even deeper into Divine Love which is the Spirit of Truth; in so doing, have a heart which is governed by Holy Love. Such a heart does not examine others' motives for their actions. The loving heart tries to avoid laying blame, for this leads to a 'tit for tat' spirit. The heart which advances in Holy Love understands that humility is the stepping stone to all virtue."

"Pray for a love of humility. Then you will advance quickly in the virtuous life."

June 29, 2002
HOLY LOVE AND HOLY HUMILITY

"I am your Jesus, born Incarnate. I have come to help you understand the Scripture passage, 'Not everyone who says—Lord, Lord—will enter the Kingdom of Heaven.' The passage goes on to say that it is those who do the Will of the Father who will enter Paradise. I tell you, there are many who practice many devotions, have many gifts of the Holy Spirit, but it is all an exterior effort. Salvation is an interior process within the human heart. Souls that do not make the effort every day to improve in Holy Love are cheating themselves, and being deceived by Satan. Such spirituality could be compared to eating a sumptuous meal, but not digesting the food. The entire purpose of the act is missed."

"Holy Love embraces every virtue, just as humility does so. Without furthering the depth of these virtues, the spirit lies stagnant. Deepening of virtue can only be accomplished in the present moment and by a movement of the free will. If you desire a deeper holiness, it will be given to you. You will be shown where you need to love more—where you need to be more humble."

"It is the souls who do not look within their own hearts that I fear for. Salvation is a moment to moment challenge in Holy Love—Holy Humility."

January 19, 2004
HOLY HUMILITY VS. PRIDE

"I am your Jesus, born Incarnate. I have come to help souls understand the virtue of humility, and to recognize in their hearts the archenemy of humility which is pride."

HUMILITY	PRIDE
...rtue.	Is a deadly sin.
...oes not see himself as holy, but sees all others as holier than himself.	Is sanctimonious – self-satisfied with where he stands before God.
Forgives others easily.	Bears grudges; sees others' faults, not his own.
Is truth.	Is Satan's lie.
Humility fosters a deepening of all other virtues. All other virtues will only be as deep as love and humility are deep in the heart.	Pride has a false sense of the depth of virtue in his heart.
Continually searches his own heart, examining it for flaws in Holy Love.	Believes he is probably in the Fifth Chamber, and there is no room for improvement.
Seeks to be hidden in the background; seeks a servant's position.	Loves to be in the limelight; seeks attention. Practices virtues for others to see.
Trusts in Jesus and in His Divine Providence.	Opens his heart to fears and doubts. Tries to control his own destiny.
Is always open to others' opinions once he has expressed his own.	Cannot surrender his own opinion; is self-righteous.
Tries in every present moment to surrender his own will to the Divine Will of God.	Cannot allow God to have His Own Way. Insists his plans, ideas and solutions are better than anything God could come up with.
Has as his motive for every thought, word and deed love of God and neighbor.	Has as a motive for every thought, word and deed self-love – his own personal agenda.

December 21, 2001
PRIDE VS. LOVE AND HUMILITY

St. Thomas Aquinas comes. He says: "Praise be to Jesus. I have come to help you understand what hinders the soul on his journey into the Chambers of the United Hearts. It is always pride. Pride is the enemy of a deeper surrender to love. The essence of pride is self-love which fosters a lack of humility. The soul does not know his place before God. He does not recognize his own faults and shortcomings. He sees his free will as the 'be all—end all'."

"You see, my little soul, humility and love must always work together in the soul. It is humility which makes Holy Love genuine

41

back to God and await the next part of God's plan with patience and forbearing."

July 21, 2005
THE CROWN OF THORNS
St. Thomas Aquinas says: "Praise be to Jesus."

"I have come to help you understand that just as every present moment is different for each person, so too, graces extended to every soul are individualized. The Crown of Thorns, in a particular way, leads the soul deeper into the virtues. This is because the Crown of Thorns, more than any part of the Passion, was a trial of humility. Humility, remember—with love—is the basis of every true virtue."

December 2, 2005
HUMILITY AND PURITY OF LOVE IN THE HEART
"I am your Jesus, born Incarnate."

"Humility will only be as deep as Holy Love is pure in the heart. In fact, the purity of love in the heart determines the depth of every virtue in every soul. Pray each day that the love in your heart becomes purer—less centered on self. Love of money and power contaminate Holy and Divine Love."

"Especially in this season of Advent, make your hearts pure—a secure dwelling place for My coming to you on Christmas."

May 5, 2006 — 12th Anniversary of Holy Love
Monthly Message to All People and Every Nation
HOLY LOVE AND HOLY HUMILITY
Jesus and Blessed Mother are here dressed in white with Their Hearts exposed. Blessed Mother says: "Praise be to Jesus." Jesus says: "I am your Jesus, born Incarnate."

Jesus: "I have come to help you see that in the spiritual realm there must be a 'marriage' between humility and love in order for the good fruit of deeper holiness to be born in the heart."

"The reason the world does not experience true and lasting peace today is that humility and love are not together in the heart of humanity. When one of these virtues is found lacking, the holiness and resulting peace are merely superficial. You cannot establish a good and sound structure on top of a faulty foundation. Therefore, understand that the soundness of your holiness depends solely on the depth of the Holy Love and Holy Humility upon which it is built."

"If you do not seek this truthful and sincere personal holiness, then you do not seek peace either. For I tell you, peace—if it is sincere—only comes from a holy heart."

"Today I tell you that without a good foundation, any structure will fall. If governments do not legislate according to the foundation of

Holy Love and humility, they will, likewise, crumble through chaos and confusion."

"With the Messages here of the spiritual journey into the Sacred Chambers of Our United Hearts, I am calling the world into a new spiritual springtime. Just as in nature, all of earth is awakening and coming forth in full bloom. I call the heart of the world to awaken to the truth of Holy and Divine Love, and to blossom in this eternal spiritual journey. Let your hearts open in littleness as tiny flowers under the feet of Eternal Love. Divine Providence does not forget those who depend on God alone. Each heart affects the heart of the world. So then, your response to Holy and Divine Love is reflected worldwide. In this spiritual journey you can be part of My Triumph, or you can call down My Justice through skepticism. Train your free will in the way of love and humility. I will help you."

"You need to remember that all advancement in technology, be it medical or industrial, comes from the Heart of your Creator. It should be used to support all life from conception to natural death. When these advancements are convoluted and used for the fulfillment of disordered self-love, you are calling My Justice down upon you."

"I have come, My brothers and sisters, to lead you into the New Jerusalem, which is one with the Triumph of Our United Hearts. In order to follow Me, you must surrender your free will to Holy and Divine Love and Holy Humility. This is the path that I choose for you."

"Today, My brothers and sisters, We are listening to all your petitions and blessing your hearts and lives with Our Blessing of the United Hearts."

August 3, 2002
PRAY TO PERFECT LOVE AND HUMILITY
"I am your Jesus, born Incarnate. Please write this down."

"Divine Heart of Jesus, in this present moment help me to live more deeply in Holy Love and Holy Humility. Give me the grace and the courage to look deep into my heart to see where I am failing in these virtues. I know it is only in overcoming these faults I can come deeper into the Chambers of Your Divine Heart. I beg Your strength in perfecting these virtues. Amen."

"Make it known."

April 17, 2006
PRAY DAILY FOR DEEPER LOVE AND HUMILITY
St. Thomas Aquinas comes and says: "Praise be to Jesus."
"I have come to help you understand that your holiness and

sanctification will only reach the depth of the humility and love in your heart. Therefore, in order to deepen your journey into the Chambers of the United Hearts, each one should pray daily for deeper love and humility, for on these two every virtue has its foundation."

"God has sent me to give you this prayer:"

"Heavenly Father, I petition Your Paternal Heart in this present moment to carry my heart deeper into Holy Love and Holy Humility. I realize that my free will must cooperate with Your Divine Will so that humility and love can increase in me".

"I give You my will now, fully accepting whatever it may please You to send me, as I choose to be a little martyr of love in Your Hands. Amen."

March 27, 1999
LESSON ON SIMPLICITY

Jesus comes with lights coming out of His wounds. He says: "I am Jesus, born Incarnate. I have come to teach you about the virtue of simplicity. Simplicity is to the soul like a compass is to a ship at sea. Simplicity keeps the soul on course, directing all thoughts, words, and actions towards God—everything in Him, with Him, and through Him."

"The simple heart holds no duplicity—no guile—no hidden agenda towards self-advantage. His words reflect what is in his heart. He seeks to please God above all else."

"If the simple soul could be seen it would be a little flower who, finding its nourishment from the sun, turns its face towards it and opens in full bloom."

"The more the soul allows himself to be steeped in self-interest, the more easily he is won over to duplicity. Perhaps he is passionate about reputation. This greatly compromises My simple call for the soul becomes compromised concerning himself about how others view him. I have My own opinion of each one. I look only into the heart. The more simple and single-hearted the soul is, the more I revel in him."

"This virtue, more than all the others, depends on Holy Love and holy humility. It is like the fruit put into the basket of love and humility. The bigger the basket—the more fruit fits in it."

"Make this known."

May 29, 2000
LESSON ON SIMPLICITY

"I am your Jesus, born Incarnate. I invite you to contemplate once again the virtue of simplicity. The simple soul allows no obstacle to

46

remain on the path between himself and God. All his thoughts, words, and actions come from a simple heart that has the singular motive of pleasing God. He is sincere and always truthful. He never tries to edify his reputation in the eyes of others through exaggeration or lies. He holds no hidden agenda in his heart towards self-advantage. He does not, in his actions, undertake projects simply to gain laud from others. He is always willing to make allowances for others' mistakes. He is always ready to forgive. Simplicity is the handrail on the staircase to holiness, for it holds the soul on the certain path of perfection."

"Make it known."

November 19, 2001
A SIMPLISTIC HEART

"I am your Jesus, born Incarnate. A simple heart is the fruit of humility. It is the pure embrace of Holy Love. In such a heart there hides no pretense or guile. Simplicity, you see, does not seek to impress men, but only to please God."

"The simplistic heart understands most clearly what is passing and what is everlasting. The obstacle to simplicity is the obstacle which stands in the way of progress into the Chambers of My Heart. It is inordinate self-love; for it is this disordered self-love that keeps the soul from surrendering to Me completely. Such a soul holds back—maybe not realizing it—but also not seeking perfect surrender."

Every present moment carries with it the grace to surrender completely—therefore, the grace to advance in holiness. But remember, each present moment also carries with it temptations against your simplistic surrender-temptations to sin."

"The more you give to Me, the more I will give to you. If you pray more, you will receive more grace to see clearly your choices between good and evil. Make this known."

November 15, 2004
SPIRITUAL CHILDHOOD—SPIRITUAL LITTLENESS

"I am your Jesus, born Incarnate."

"I have come to help you understand the importance of spiritual childhood—spiritual littleness. The child seeks only to please his parent—to appeal to his parent. In a similar way, the spiritually little seek only to satisfy the Will of God. They want to be in the presence of God more than anything. If they feel they are displeasing God in any way, they quickly seek His forgiveness. It is impossible to become spiritually little outside of humility and love. So, for this reason alone, spiritual littleness is a necessary step to perfection and to the journey through the Chambers of Our United Hearts."

"Please make this known."

November 15, 2004
PRAY TO EMBRACE SPIRITUAL LITTLENESS

"I am your Jesus, born Incarnate."

"I am giving you this prayer to help you to embrace spiritual littleness:"

"Dear Jesus, I wish to come to you as a little child. As a child, I desire only to appeal to you. In this effort, I reject the pomp of the world. I embrace the truth of humility which reveals to me where I am in God's Eyes. I seek only God's approval in every present moment."

"Thus I surrender my own will and my human nature to the Divine Will of God. In doing so, I do not chase after pleasures or importance in human eyes. I allow God complete mastery over my heart, trusting always in His plans for me. Amen."

June 7, 2006
SPIRITUAL LITTLENESS

"I am your Jesus, born Incarnate."

"Spiritual littleness comes only as the soul surrenders to humility and self-effacement. Therefore, understand that it is a cooperation between grace and human effort that results in childlike littleness."

"Those who seek to be recognized as holy are opposing the grace of littleness with their free will. They are, in fact, deep into spiritual pride. Those who are self-righteous will never be little in My Eyes, for they are making gods of their own opinions. Those who hold grudges are allowing unforgiveness to become like a god. If they ask Me, I will help them to forgive."

"Spiritual littleness requires humble surrender, humble trust and complete self-effacement, making all others more important than self. It is not easy, but in My Eyes—a perfection in Holy and Divine Love."

November 8, 2006
THE DEPTH OF HUMILITY, SIMPLICITY, AND LOVE

"I am your Jesus, born Incarnate."

"Remember, it is impossible to reach the depths of My Heart outside of humility, simplicity and love. The souls that lose sight of this, slip from the path of Holy Love. The depth of every virtue is in proportion to the depth of these three—humility, love and simplicity. Holy Love is the key that unlocks the door to the other two—humility and simplicity."

April 11, 2007
CHILDLIKE SIMPLICITY AND LOVE

"I am your Jesus, born Incarnate."

"I invite you to understand that only the childlike can surrender to Me without reserve. In simplicity the childlike are able to trust with their whole heart in the fullness of Holy Love. The child has no guile, no hidden agenda, no self-love to block the path of My grace. Therefore, it is in childlikeness the soul can best initiate Divine Love."

April 16, 2007
HAVE A SINGULAR HEART

Jesus and Blessed Mother are here with Their Hearts exposed. Blessed Mother says: "Praise be to Jesus." Jesus says: "I am your Jesus, born Incarnate."

Jesus: "My brothers and sisters, My best advice to each one of you is to have a singular heart living only in Holy and Divine Love, proceeding deeper into Our Hearts through simplicity. In this way your burdens will be lightened, your crosses made bearable, your victories numerous; and I will be with you always."

Blessed Mother...

Jesus: "We're blessing you with Our Blessing of the United Hearts.

PRAYER FOR HUMILITY

"Dear Jesus, recreate my heart today in humility. Let my every thought, word, and deed be for your greater honor and glory, never my own. Show me the areas of pride in my life and help me to overcome my pride. I ask this in Your Most Holy Name, Lord Jesus. Amen."

Love, Compassion and Forgiveness

September 5, 1996
HOLY LOVE AND HOLY COMPASSION ARE INSEPARABLE

Jesus: "My Mercy and My Love are inseparable. Holy Love and Holy Compassion are inseparable. You need to always forgive and overlook each other's faults. Work on your own holiness. I call those who will serve. Remember, I do not call the perfect but the willing."

April 10, 2006
COMPASSION LOOKS FOR THE GOOD IN OTHERS

"I am your Jesus born Incarnate."

"Today I invoke you, do not be quick to examine the faults of others though they be real and present. Look, rather, for the good in each person for the Holy Love they manifest in word and deed. This is the compassionate way to regard one another. If it is your duty to correct someone, do so in Holy Love."

December 9, 1998
LESSON ON UNFORGIVENESS

Our Lady comes as Refuge of Holy Love. She is seated on a throne and in a pink light. She says: "Praised be Jesus. My angel, today I come to you once again seeking reconciliation between all people, all nations, and God. As I have revealed to you, judging each other is the first step to unforgiveness. Now please understand, the last step in unforgiveness, that is the most unmerciful outward sign against another, is persecution. The unborn are persecuted in the womb for who they are and what they will become. Races and nationalities are persecuted in much the same way. The Church and other religions face an ongoing battle against persecutors. I, Myself, am persecuted by those whom I love. Persecution is unloving, unforgiving, unaccepting, misunderstanding, and uncompassionate— all taken together as one."

"It should not surprise you, then, that My missionaries and seers are also considered fair game for Satan's persecution. Much evil is accomplished in the name of discernment. Discernment needs to be accomplished through prayer and openness to the truth. Some take pride in opposing the ones I use. This is persecution as well."

"All wars and insurrections begin in judging, then unforgiveness, and finally, persecution."

"See, then, what an unkind act unforgiveness is. See what it leads to. It leads to hate—the opposite of Holy Love."

"Please search your hearts today, My children, for any area of unforgiveness, of judging, or persecution. I am blessing you."

LESSON ON UNFORGIVENESS

Finding fault	Compassion
⇓	⇓
Judgment	Compassion
⇓	⇓
Unforgiveness	Compassion
⇓	⇓
Persecution	Compassion
⇓	⇓
Hate	Love

February 20, 1999
LESSON ON FORGIVENESS

"I am Jesus, born Incarnate. I have come to share with you a lesson on forgiveness. To be forgiving the soul must first be loving. This is an obvious base on which forgiveness is built. Unforgiveness is an overpowering obstacle to holiness. It keeps the heart centered on self and not God or neighbor. Since self-love is the root of all sin, it is at the very basis of all unforgiveness."

"This is why the soul cannot surrender to Me past hurts, for he puts his own feelings first—God and all others last."

"I showed compassion to those who wronged Me. But for so many, it is too much of a challenge to their love and humility to return love and forgiveness for insult and injury. You must love Me more than you love yourself. I have commanded it. Forgiveness is a sign that you have done so and are well on the way of holiness. Unforgiveness tells Me you allow your heart to center on you—your pride, your injury. Do not say, 'Why me?' Do not think, 'Woe is me, such and such happened to me.' Such thoughts are full of self-love and bear unforgiveness as a fruit."

"I send you the grace, through My Mother's Heart, that you need to forgive. Open your hearts. Receive it. Welcome it."

"Receive the benediction of My Heart in your lives."

July 31, 2004
HOLY FORGIVENESS

"I am your Jesus, born Incarnate. I have come so that you will know that the soul who forgives all his enemies, his persecutors and detractors is a soul who is blameless in My sight. It is such as these that advance quickly through the Chambers of Our United Hearts. This is Holy Forgiveness and can only be accomplished through Holy Love."

"When the soul asks with a sincere heart, he receives My assistance in reaching this depth of forgiveness. This is not to say that he no longer holds unpleasant memories about certain people in his past, but he can recall these people and situations without anger. Anger and unforgiveness go hand in hand."

"Upon this journey of forgiveness, the soul begins to pray for the ones who have in some way injured him. The more unforgiveness is overcome in the heart, the more I fill the heart with My Divine Love— Divine Mercy. The soul must realize that this inner healing cannot take place in his heart apart from Holy Love, for it is love which must replace bitterness and anger."

"Tantamount to forgiving is to recognize the need to forgive."

"You will please make this known."

August 9, 2004
UNFORGIVENESS

"I am your Jesus, Divine Love—Divine Mercy, born Incarnate."

"I have come to speak to you once again about unforgiveness. If love and mercy combined made a fine sauce, unforgiveness would be like a bitter herb that ruined the chef's masterpiece when he added it. Unforgiveness in the soul is like a deadly disease—insidious at the onset, but as a deadly cancer to every virtue."

"Resentments and woundedness are unforgiveness. These are like introverted anger. These are a form of pride buried deep within the soul eating away at personal holiness. Resentments and woundedness come from disordered self-love. The soul cannot accept the wrong that was done to him as God's permitting Will. He cannot allow God to weave the tapestry of his own salvation. He cannot meet the challenge of becoming more humble."

"I invite each one to surrender everything in the past to Me. Accept all the insults others have perpetrated against you with humility. This is how you surrender to forgiveness. Accept your own sinfulness and weaknesses. I do—I still love you and I forgive you!"

April 20, 2007
PURSUE FORGIVENESS INTELLECTUALLY,
EMOTIONALLY AND SPIRITUALLY

St. Thomas Aquinas says: "Praise be to Jesus."

"Please realize that every virtue must be pursued intellectually, emotionally and spiritually; otherwise it is only pretense. Forgiveness is no different. If it is pursued in the mind and with emotion, it is a beginning."

"But the real virtue of forgiveness must be deep in the heart. In like manner, the soul must not allow unforgiveness to enter his intellect and emotions. To do so assails the forgiveness he may have accepted in his heart. This is how Satan attacks the virtuous heart."

Faith, Hope, Love, Trust, Surrender and Peace

March 19, 2001
FAITH – HOPE – LOVE – TRUST

"I am your Jesus, born Incarnate. The soul who trusts in Me is deep into the virtues of faith, hope and love, for it is these three that bear the fruit of trust. Faith is trust in action and belief in the Intangible. Hope is trust in God's Provision in the future. Love—being the basis of every virtue, the light that shines through every virtue—is the basis and fiber of trust. You cannot love Me if you do not trust Me. You cannot trust Me if you do not first love Me."

"Make it known."

July 24, 1999
LESSON ON FAITH

"I am your Jesus, born Incarnate. My sister, allow Me to offer you some thoughts on faith. Faith is like the rock, which is unmoving and unchanged as the tempest sweeps by it. It is like the nail that holds secure the frame of a house. The degree of faith in the heart when a prayer is offered is like the heat in an oven. The warmer the oven the more quickly and completely the bread is baked. The higher the degree of faith, the more quickly and completely a prayer is answered."

"Faith is like gold which surrounds a great jewel, protecting it and revealing its splendor to the world. The gold is your faith, and the jewel your salvation. Faith is the path that leads you along the way of love with perseverance."

"Without faith you are tossed about like the branches of a tree in a windstorm. Like the branch, your heart cannot settle or be at peace."

"Faith is like the wind that supports a kite in the spring breeze. If the breeze stops, the kite (your soul) sinks to the ground."

"Petition My Heart for faith. Always ask for a deeper faith. Faith, like love, can never be given in over-abundance."

"My peace be with you." He leaves.

January 9, 2003
EXPECTANT FAITH

St. Thomas Aquinas comes. He says: "Praise be to Jesus."

"You can accomplish much more through faith and hope than you can through doubts and discouragement. It is important that your petitions rise from a heart full of expectant faith, for such confidence in God's good plans will not be overlooked by grace. Understanding this is a step towards every goal."

June 26, 1999
LESSON ON HOPE

Jesus comes with His Heart exposed. He says, "I am your Jesus, born Incarnate. Today, I will address the virtue of hope. Hope is faith and love in action. Hope is like a fisherman casting his net into the sea. He has faith that there are fish in the sea. If he casts his nets with Holy Love in his heart, he is able to hope that the Loving God will bless his catch."

"Those who hope in the world or in mortal efforts aside from God will always be disappointed. Holy hope allows you to trust in God's Provision and His Divine Will for you. Holy Hope motivates your surrender to God—your self-abandonment. Holy Hope lets you trust in God's Mercy."

"Holy Hope is like the farmer who, planting his crop, builds a great silo in hopes of a bountiful harvest. So too are you hopeful when you sacrifice and suffer, thus laying up for yourselves heavenly treasure."

"Those that hope in the Lord, trust in me as well. Those that pray with hopeful hearts receive all they need and much more besides."

"If you do not love, you cannot trust. If you do not trust, you cannot hope. All the virtues blossom from a heart rooted in Holy Love."

"Make it known."

May 30, 2001
HAVE HOPE

"I am your Jesus, born Incarnate. I come today to invite you to have hope. If hope were a balloon rising in the air, doubt and fear would be the pin that would burst it. Hope is a fruit of trust—trust a fruit of love."

"Suppose you hope in something that is not in God's Will for you. Your hope is still a joy to Me, for it is an expression of your love. Believe that I desire only the best for you, and hope in Me."

November 23, 2006
PRAY WITH A HOPEFUL HEART

"I am your Jesus, born Incarnate."

"Today I have come to ask you to always pray with the garment of hope over your heart. Hope stems from Holy Love and faith. It is surrounded by love and faith. It is the hopeful petition that is carried deepest into My Heart."

"Hope does not allow the mist of fear to consume it. Hope is courageous and thankful—ever seeking to see My Father's Will in the present moment. Hope comes to you through the Heart of My Mother as a gift in the midst of turmoil. Hope is the remedy for despair."

"My Heart turns towards the hopeful heart, making it steadfast and persevering. Hope is the foundation of fortitude."

September 22, 2002
HOPE VS. PRESUMPTION *(PART 1)*

St. Thomas Aquinas comes. He bows to the tabernacle saying: "Praise be to Jesus. I have come to help you understand the difference between presumption and hope. They are opposites."

"Presumption takes for granted—grace. The presumptuous person thinks he has what he does not have. He does not allow in his heart space for the action of God's Divine Will. He would be like a ship caught in a turbulent sea that thinks he is safely docked."

"Hope, on the other hand, is a virtue that practices expectant faith. The hopeful person believes God can accomplish anything if it is His Will to do so. He entrusts his needs and petitions to the Lord, and allows Him to answer as He wills. In hope, he may even thank God ahead of time for whatever the Divine decision may be. The difference is—he does not presume the answer to his petition. His would be the ship lost at sea—praying with expectant faith to find a safe harbor."

"It is quite important to realize that Satan can mimic any gift of the Holy Spirit. The presumptuous person believes every inspiration to be from God, and does not test the spirit. Remember, the only virtue Satan cannot imitate is humility, for he does not even understand it. So, in humility, be certain that you do not presume you have a certain gift or virtue."

September 22, 2002
HOPE VS. PRESUMPTION *(PART 2)*

St. Thomas Aquinas comes. He bows towards me saying:

"Praise be to Jesus ever present in your little heart when you are embracing Holy Love."

"I have come once again to discuss with you the difference between hope and presumption."

"The virtue of hope proceeds from a heart full of Holy Love, Holy Humility and Holy Trust. Such a heart is able to hope based on the faith that God desires only that which is best for him."

"Presumption is based on pride. The presumptuous soul regards all things through the eyes of disordered self-love. He may presume he will be saved even though he leads an unrepentant life of sin. He believes he will receive salvation on his own terms, not God's terms. Such a soul trusts only in himself and makes no allowance for God's Will."

"There are those in the world today—indeed in places of prominence—who believe they have certain virtues or even certain gifts of the Holy Spirit. But, once again I tell you that which is not based on humility of heart is Satan's counterfeit."

May 9, 2005
HOPE VS. DISCOURAGEMENT
Jesus and Blessed Mother are here with Their Hearts exposed. Blessed Mother says: "Praise be to Jesus."

Jesus: "I am your Jesus, born Incarnate. My brothers and sisters, never allow discouragement to be a part of your heart; rather, have hope always, for hope comes from the Lord. The Father desires that you unite your will to His, and this is only possible if you overcome the obstacle of discouragement that Satan sets upon you."

"Every moment holds precious grace with which to be victorious. Therefore, live in joy, hope and peace, and always trust that the victory is Ours."

"We're blessing you with Our Blessing of the United Hearts."

January 24, 2007
FAITH – HOPE – LOVE – TRUST
"I am your Jesus, born Incarnate."

"Please understand that faith, hope and love bear the fruit of trust. Without trust, they are superficial. Trust is only as strong as these three—faith, hope and love."

June 25, 2000
FAITH, TRUST AND LOVE
"I am your Jesus, born Incarnate. My sister, I tell you faith and trust go together. One is not present in the soul apart from the other. And neither can exist outside of love. If faith were a ship sailing on the sea, trust would be the ballast keeping it afloat. The little rudder which would direct the ship of faith and trust would be love."

"Make it known."

July 17, 2004
HOLY LOVE AND HOLY TRUST
"I am your Jesus, born Incarnate. I have come to tell you that greater merit is earned through trust than any other single virtue. I say this, for love and trust are the same. Holy Love and Holy Trust are always coupled and they are the embodiment of every other virtue. No one can trust Me who does not love Me. No one can say they love Me who does not also trust in Me."

"Those who worry or fear for any reason should understand they need to be purified through a deeper perfection in Holy Love."

August 10, 1998
TRUST IN GOD'S PROVISION

Jesus: "I have come to describe to you the great love I have for those who trust in My Provision. Those who trust and have confidence in Me will receive in this life My support and companionship in all their efforts. I will not abandon them. I will keep them in peace. In heaven I will place them at the foot of My throne, seated beside the saints who embraced My Father's Will, and those who have consecrated themselves to the Heart of My Mother. You see trust as a small thing. I tell you, it is all."

February 13, 1999
LESSON ON TRUST

"Ah! You have come at last." *(Delayed by snow.)* "I am Jesus, your Savior—the Word made Flesh. I have come to speak to you today about trust."

"As I have told you, the path that leads you to Divine Love—My Sacred Heart—is Holy Love. If your soul is not steeped in Holy Love, you cannot approach the door to My heart. The key which unlocks the door of this Heart is trustful surrender. The more you surrender to My Provision—the more I know you love Me. Trust is the key that looses [*i.e. to let loose or release*] the grace of My Provision. Confidence allows the soul to taste peace and to accept the Will of God."

"Every journey has some obstacle. The path to holiness is no different. Obstacles which stand in the way of your holiness are the same ones that keep you from trustful surrender."

"Perhaps you trust only yourself through self-love. A fruit of this flaw is fear. You try to control and manipulate the people around you. Maybe you dominate every conversation and refuse to let go of your opinion. Why? If you surrender all things to Me, I will attend perfectly to your every need."

"Perhaps you trust only in other people and pray only when others fail you. Trust Me always. My Provision is perfect."

"If you are like a little child, you will earn the Kingdom of Heaven, for a child places all his trust in his parents. Likewise, you must trust in Me."

"If the grace of My Heart were a beautiful bouquet of flowers, trust would be the gentle breeze that would carry the fragrance to you."

"Trust is like ascending a mountain; the higher you get, the closer you are to Heaven."

"Even in your trials, you must trust Me if you desire holiness. Nothing is permitted in your life that does not lead you close to Me, if you trust."

He leaves.

TRUST IN GOD'S PROVISION	LACK OF TRUST
Rapid progression in life of virtue.	−Flaws in Holy Love −Flaws in Holy Humility
Loves God and trusts Him above all else.	−Much Self-Love −Fear −Learns to depend on people, but not God
Lives in Divine Love and Divine Will.	−Cannot accept God's Will −Seeks a reason for everything that happens to him

February 26, 1999
PRAY TO LEARN THE VALUE OF TRUST

"I am Jesus, born Incarnate. I desire each soul learn the value of trust. Here is a prayer:

"Dear Jesus, teach me to trust only in the power of You, Your Father, and the Holy Spirit. I surrender my will to You. In this surrender I accept that Your grace controls the future. I understand that You love me and want only my good—my salvation. I resolve to live in the present and await whatever You may plan for me in the future. I will trust in Your plans and Divine Will for me. Amen."

October 11, 2000 — Conversation with Divine Love
TRUST AND PRAYER PETITIONS

"I am your Jesus, born Incarnate. I have come to you today to speak about trust. The depth of your trust in Me is the proving ground of the depth of faith, hope, love, and humility in your heart. I look at the amount of trust in the heart as I consider each prayer petition. The petition steeped in the deepest trust is the one surrendered completely to Me. This is the most worthy petition and the one I act upon with the fullness of My Grace and Mercy."

"The proud heart is unable to offer Me such a prayer for such a heart trusts only in his own efforts. He looks to control each situation and seeks My assistance in this control. He is unwilling to surrender to the Divine Will and Divine Provision."

"The proud heart hopes only within the confines of his own will—his wants and his needs. He cannot accept Heaven's solution. Thus, he shows Me that he loves his own will more than Me. He has faith in his own plans and solutions—not in My Own. The proud heart trusts himself and lays divided before Me. Such a one is easily conquered by Satan."

"This is why I place such great value on trust in Me. The soul's trust is proof of his love for Me. It is the measure of his humility. It is the barometer of his faith and hope. The one who trusts in Me draws upon the greatest abundance of My Mercy and Love. Thus am I able to minister with the most attentive care to his needs."

"Make this known."

September 25, 2006 — Conversation with Divine Love
TRUST AND PRAYER PETITIONS (PART 1)

"I am your Jesus, born Incarnate."

"Child, place everything—every problem, every petition—in the recesses of My Divine Heart. Herein, all is attended to according to the Divine Will of My Eternal Father. Nothing is forgotten or overlooked. Nothing is unimportant. Whatever concerns you, concerns Me, as well. Every solution is within My Sacred Heart; nothing goes unanswered. Trust—yes, childlike trust—is what holds all your petitions in My Heart. When you can turn everything over to Me and to the welfare of My Heart, then My actions in your life are most profound and powerful."

September 29, 2006 — Conversation with Divine Love
TRUST AND PRAYER PETITIONS (PART 2)

"I am your Jesus, born Incarnate."

"To continue My discussion with you on trust. As it is the 'hand of trust' that holds your petitions in My Sacred Heart, I act promptly in strengthening and supporting the trust you show Me by placing My Wounded Hand under your hand. Thus, we act together in this effort of trust."

"Your initial effort of prayerfully surrendering each petition to My Heart is secured in place with your trust in My Provision. When I see your trust, I come to your aid, and support you by merit of My own woundedness."

May 22, 1999
SELF-SURRENDER

"I am your Jesus, Divine Love, born Incarnate. I have come to explain to you the fullness of My call, which is self-surrender. Without your surrender I cannot achieve in you My goal and your salvation. Surrender means that you must give up or relinquish something. Self-surrender is My call for you to give up your own will. Your will is directed by whatever is in your heart in the present moment. This is why My call to self-surrender is at once My call to complete submission to Holy Love in the present moment."

"Self-surrender is the key that unlocks the door to My Heart and to Divine Providence. So often you do not see My Provision because you are blinded by what you want. So often what you want is not good for you and will not lead to your salvation."

"My provision, My Divine Will for you, is like a great tapestry that I, the Weaver, begin to weave at your conception. All through your life, I design to put each thread in its place to create the masterpiece of your salvation. When you refuse to surrender to Me, you inasmuch as pull a thread out of place. Then I, the Artist, must redesign the entire tapestry so that it all comes together harmoniously. But when you surrender to Me, the final outcome is much more easily attainable. You see My grace and you cooperate with My provision, My plan. The design is more beautiful because it is My best design."

"Your self-surrender is what moves your feet up the staircase of holiness. Your surrender lets you inhale the sweet fragrance of the bouquet of My grace. Without your surrender you are like a broken tool in the hands of a master carpenter. The carpenter cannot use such a tool, so he sets it aside and searches out a better one. In the same way, I cannot use you to the fullest unless you surrender completely to Me."

"When you surrender, you are telling Me you trust Me to lead you, guide you, provide for you, protect you. I cannot resist such a one. My love completely embraces such a soul and I am united with him. This is why I tell you, your trust is everything. Your trust is your surrender."

March 7, 2001
HOLY INDIFFERENCE

"I am your Jesus, born Incarnate. Receive this message with a loving heart for I, your Lord, speak it. When you surrender it means you have a Holy Indifference as to the outcome of a situation. This is the nugget of truth that allows you to live in conformity to the Divine Will."

"Surrender is always surrounded by trust. You trust that God has an infinite, eternal plan that will bring good from any turn of events. Therefore, you remain indifferent as to the outcome, knowing God, who is Love, will engineer the best outcome. Even when I was lost in the Temple, My Mother surrendered the outcome to God. She knew, full well, He had a plan and She accepted this plan blindly in trust."

"In order to trust the soul must be humble and loving. If these two virtues are not in the heart, every other virtue will be superficial— false. I see through every pretense. I will not help the proud soul to surrender. I bend down to the lowly and assist them in their needs."

"Make this known."

October 16, 2000
TRUSTFUL SURRENDER IS THE KEY

Jesus, Blessed Virgin Mary, and St. Margaret Mary Alacoque appear. Blessed Mother and St. Margaret Mary say, "Praise be to Jesus." Jesus says, "I am your Jesus, born Incarnate." Blessed Mother says: "Now we have come full circle."

Jesus: "I have come to explain to you the completeness of the Revelation revealed through you. All of what Heaven would reveal began with the Key to the Immaculate Heart of Mary—the Prayer to Mary, Protectress of the Faith. This simple prayer admits the soul into the First Chamber of Our United Hearts, which is the Immaculate Heart of Mary. With faith protected and Satan laid waste, the soul opens his heart to Holy Love—the First Chamber of the United Hearts."

"One year ago I revealed to you the inner Chambers of My Sacred Heart, which is the completion of the United Hearts Revelation and the spiritual journey towards perfection."

"The key to the innermost Chambers of My Heart is trustful surrender. Without this, the soul cannot come deeper into My Heart of Hearts. Therefore, see that the depth of trust in the heart is also the depth of holiness. The soul that does not love Me cannot trust Me. The soul that does not trust Me cannot surrender his will to Me. It is that simple and that complex."

"Once I said to you that you see trust as a 'sometimes thing'. Your trust must be always—amidst conflict and victory. Trust Me no matter what. I am God. There is nothing that befalls you that I am not aware of. All things turn to good for those who love Me. (Romans Chapter 8). Even in the cross is My victory."

"Acceptance of the cross and acceptance of God's Will are one in the same. But you can accept neither of these if you do not love Me, trust Me and surrender your will to Me."

"My plans are beyond your own, My Father's Will for you higher than you can imagine. When you trustingly surrender to Me, We can work together. It is then I take you deepest into the Chambers of My Heart and your weakness is transformed by My strength."

"Yes, your trust is everything. It is a reflection of your innermost being."

"Please make this known."

August 29, 2001
TRUSTFUL SURRENDER THROUGH LOVE

St. Thomas Aquinas is here. He says: "Praise be to Jesus. You question how you achieve this elusive trustful surrender through love. First and foremost, love Jesus with your whole heart. Then accept whatever He sends you in every present moment. This means, dear one, you grow to love the Will of God. When you make plans, if God sends a different plan, you embrace it, all the while knowing His plan is best for you."

"Let me show you the opposite of trustful surrender through love. This would be a person who cannot let go of his wants. He sets goals and does not want God to have His say. He cannot give up control and be indifferent as to the outcome of a situation. This way of thinking says to Jesus and the Father: 'I love my will, not Yours'."

"Do you see the difference? Trustful surrender through love takes a humble stand—always waiting and watching for God's Will."

"Try to assimilate what I have told you today. Pray for the grace to do so."

January 26, 2002
SANCTITY THROUGH TRUSTFUL SURRENDER

St. Thomas Aquinas comes. He says: "Praise be to Jesus. My sister, this is the whole and the sum of sanctification—trustful surrender to the Divine Will of God in every present moment. In this trust is love. In this surrender is humility. In love, humility and conformity to God's Will is self-denial."

"The soul who reaches for sanctity must completely surrender what he wants for what God wants. He puts God in the center of his heart and roots out self. It is impossible for the one who is self-absorbed to reach the heights of this surrender, for he views everything as to how it affects himself. He looks for self-gain in everything. He trusts in himself more than in God, for his love of God is imperfect. His existence revolves around his own welfare and not what God wills for him."

"The soul who pursues sanctification, however, tries to accept all things as from the Hand of God. He sees God's Will in every situation. He understands that God is working with him, drawing him into sanctification. Therefore, he does not see God's Will as a sharp edged sword, but as a blazing beam of light illuminating the path he is called to follow."

"Inordinate self-love cannot choose Divine Love, for the two conflict just as the flesh opposes the spirit. But this Message of the Chambers of the United Hearts calls each one to take off the old and put on the new. This is the essence of sanctity."

September 9, 2002
"JESUS, I TRUST IN YOU"

"I am your Jesus, born Incarnate. I have come so that you may know your greatest gift to Me is your trust in Me; for in your trust is your love for Me. The depth of your trust in Me is in direct proportion of the depth of your love of Me. Therefore, when you pray the little prayer—'*Jesus, I trust in You*'—with profound love in your heart,

My merciful gaze rests upon you. My Heart opens and the torrent of grace within It floods your soul. I can refuse no one My attentive gaze when they pray thus."

"Please make this known."

November 14, 2001
DEPTH OF TRUST

St. Thomas Aquinas comes. He says: "Praise be to Jesus."

"I have come to help you comprehend why Jesus beseeches your trust in Him daily. It is because the depth of your trust reflects the depth of your love. Trust is the barometer of your love. When you have deep sentiments of love for someone, you welcome the opportunity to demonstrate your trust in him. When you trust you place your faith in him. It is a grace, then, to be given the opportunity to trust, for it is a way of showing your love and affection."

"On the other hand you must see attacks against trust as either human weakness or evil inspiration. Oppose these thoughts by invoking Mary, Protectress of the Faith and Refuge of Holy Love."

February 28, 2007
TRUST IN THE FATHER'S LOVING WILL

Once again I see a great Flame surrounding the tabernacle. I know It to be the Heart of God the Father. He says: "Praise be to Jesus truly present in the tabernacles of the world."

"Dear child, no one can fathom the depths of My Divine Will any more than they can fathom My Divine Mercy. But in the same way that Jesus petitions your heart to trust in Divine Mercy, I beg your trust in My Divine Will. Remember, trust is the fruit of love. Therefore, pray for a deep and abiding love of My Divine Will for you."

"Do not be quick to question circumstances and events of the day, but see My Will in every present moment. Carry in your heart and upon your lips, the ejaculation, *'Eternal Father, I trust in Your loving Will for me.'* This little prayer carries with it—peace. I send an angel to assist you when you believe."

"I, your Eternal Father, desire this be made known and be made popular."

March 2, 2007
ACCEPT THE FATHER'S LOVING WILL

"I am your Jesus, born Incarnate."

"Now this is the way to accept the Divine Will of the Father. Surrender yourself completely to Me. I cannot lead you or provide anything for you outside of the Father's loving Divine Will. Just as Divine Love and Divine Mercy are one, so too, are the Will of My Father and My Will. His Heart is inseparable from My Own Sacred

Heart. Therefore, when you abandon your own will for what I desire, you are surrendering to My Father's Will for you."

March 19, 2001
FEAR VS. TRUST
The Holy Spirit showed Maureen the following vision:

INORDINATE SELF-LOVE EQUALS FEAR	FAITH, HOPE AND LOVE EQUALS TRUST
Much anxiety over future. Much guilt over past.	Surrenders future to God's Provision, and past to God's Mercy.
Unable to surrender to Divine Will. Hangs on to anger, grudges, opinions and reputation; also love of material things.	Give everything to God. *"Fear is useless. What is needed is trust."* Mark 5:36
Misses opportunities of grace in the present moment.	Perfects the virtue of love in his heart in the present moment. *"Perfect love casts out all fear."* 1 John 4:18

November 26, 2001
LACK OF TRUST
St. Thomas Aquinas comes. He says: "Praise be to Jesus. I have come to help you understand that since trust is the substance of your love of God as Jesus has revealed to you, it is lack of trust that opens the abyss between the soul and his Creator. What causes a heart to mistrust or falter in trust in God's Divine Plan, especially souls that are tethered securely to the Heart of their Savior through Divine Love?"

"First of all the soul fails to recognize that God's Will is also in the test of trust. The Lord tests each one's trust in Him as a way of strengthening the soul's love of Him. Secondly, the soul in the midst of the test begins to trust himself and his own efforts more than any plan God may have."

"This is pride based on fear and insecurity. Begin, then, to see every trial is a test of your trust. If you persevere in trust through the assistance of grace, your love of God will be strengthened. If, however, you pull back through mistrust, the trial will be greater, and in the end such a soul will be weaker in his love of God."

January 18, 2007
TRUST VS. LACK OF TRUST

Maureen had a vision of the following:

TRUSTING SOUL	SOUL WHO LACKS TRUST
Believes in God's Love and Mercy upon him.	Is unable to feel God's Love and Mercy. Feels guilty over past sin. Trusts only human effort.
Heart is centered on God and others. Lives in Holy Love.	Self-centered. Views everything as how it effects self. Many flaws oppose Holy Love.
Open to illumination of conscience. Always seeks to improve. Welcomes criticism.	Is insulted when others suggest he has a fault. Defensive. Does not easily accept correction.
Tries to find good in others.	Is judgmental. Looks for others' faults.

Lack of trust is a pride which places human limitations on God. Such a soul does not accept wholeheartedly the messages, but judges, instead of discerns.

Outline of Satan's Assault on Free Will

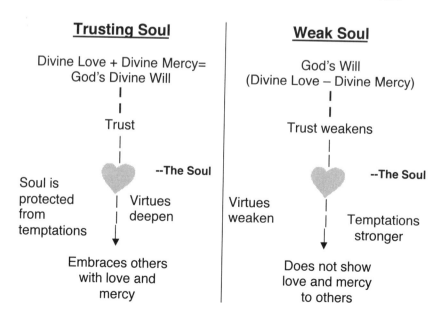

Trusting Soul	Weak Soul
Divine Love + Divine Mercy= God's Divine Will	God's Will (Divine Love – Divine Mercy)
Trust	Trust weakens
--The Soul	--The Soul
Soul is protected from temptations	Virtues deepen	Virtues weaken	Temptations stronger
Embraces others with love and mercy	Does not show love and mercy to others

June 12, 2003
HOLY TRUST VS. WORLDLY TRUST

"I am your Jesus, born Incarnate. In the world trust in Divine Providence is mere folly. For the world trusts that which it can experience only with the senses. But to the spiritually wise, trust in the Divine Provision of My Sacred Heart is the path of fulfillment, rich in promise, enduring in consolation."

"Do not waste a moment in worry. Worry is one of Satan's traps that he uses to capture the present moment for himself. Rather, let the present moment be sealed forever in faith, hope and love. Then I will bless you abundantly."

January 10, 2007
HOW SATAN ATTACKS TRUST

"I am your Jesus, born Incarnate."

"My messenger, I have told you in the past that your trust in Me is a barometer of the depth of your love for Me. This is how Satan attacks trust. He convinces the soul that everything depends on human effort. The soul no longer sees that I am present and concerned for every detail in their life. He no longer lives in trustful surrender to the Divine Will."

"Remember, the Divine Will is comprised of Divine Love and Divine Mercy. So the soul that has difficulty in trust, also has difficulty in accepting that God loves him and forgives him. Then it follows that he is not practicing love and forgiveness towards others."

"This is the spiritual destruction that Satan pursues in every soul. When the enemy can successfully separate the soul from a trustful relationship with Me, he is free to attack the soul through the many weaknesses he may fall prey to."

"Therefore, beware of any weakness in trust or any camouflage Satan uses that sets you about trusting too much in your own efforts."

March 25, 2007
GUILT, ANXIETY AND WORRY

Jesus is here, all in white. He says: "I am your Jesus, born Incarnate."

"Today, My brothers and sisters, you must realize that Satan is trying every inroad into your hearts to destroy your peace. He is the Father of Lies—the master deceiver and unrelenting accuser."

"The devil tries to rob you of the present moment through guilt, anxiety and worry. These three—guilt, anxiety and worry—are always the enemy's attack on your trustful surrender to the Divine Will of My Father. My Father's Will is Pure Mercy—Pure Love."

"When Satan is able to weaken your trust in the Divine Will, he strengthens his grip on your heart and weakens your journey into Holy and Divine Love."

"Today, My brothers and sisters, realize that there are many obstacles that can come between your heart and Mine. Your heart can be divided by love of the world, love of reputation, love of your appearance; but these, for certain, are the greatest weapons Satan uses—guilt, anxiety and worry. With these he destroys your trust and your love of Me and of the Divine Will. Therefore, stand guard over your heart and recognize his attacks."

"I'm blessing you with My Blessing of Divine Love."

March 26, 2007 – Feast of the Annunciation
BLESSED MOTHER'S EXAMPLE OF TRUST

Jesus and Blessed Mother are here. They are both in white with Their Hearts exposed. Blessed Mother says: "Praise be to Jesus." Jesus says: "I am your Jesus, born Incarnate."

Jesus: "Today, My brothers and sisters, the Church celebrates the Feast of the Annunciation. I invite you to reflect upon the trust that was in My Mother's Heart when the Angel Gabriel visited Her. I remind you that the trust in your heart reflects the depth of love in your heart. Do not lose sight of this, and do not allow Satan to attack trust through guilt, worry and anxiety. When your trust falters, your relationship with Me falters. Therefore, remain steadfast in Holy Love."

"We're blessing you with Our Blessing of the United Hearts."

March 27, 2007
SATAN'S ATTACKS ON TRUST

St. Thomas Aquinas says: "Praise be to Jesus."

"Today, I will, so to speak, sum up what the Lord has been telling you about trust. Trust is the barometer of the depth of Holy and Divine Love in the heart. Satan attacks trust through worry, anxiety and guilt. Through these weapons, he attacks trust in God's Divine Provision and trust in the Lord's Divine Mercy."

"When there is a breach in trust, the soul's relationship with God is weakened. Then Satan has an opening to launch his attacks with every sort of temptation—temptations against faith, hope and love—temptations towards discouragement, impatience, envy. All of his temptations can only be as strong as the lack of trust in the heart, which is in direct proportion to the lack of Holy Love in the heart."

"So you see the importance of trust."

March 12, 2001
LOVE – TRUST – SURRENDER – PEACE

"Thank you for coming. I have awaited your arrival. I am your Jesus, born Incarnate."

"I have spoken much to you in this penitential season of Lent about surrender—surrender of your own will—surrender to the Divine Will of God. Understand that your will and your wants are the same. Because you see the future with human eyes, that is, imperfectly— what you want may not be what God sees you need. You were created to know and love God, and to share eternity with Me. Your wants very well may not lead you to this end. But the Will of My Father is perfect, eternal and all-encompassing. How foolish not to trust in His Will for you, then. If you do not trust it is because you do not love as you should. Love is the virtue that shines through every virtue, especially trust."

"The soul that trusts only in himself—his wants and his efforts—is like a ship without a rudder cast about on the sea of self-love. It is tossed upon the waves of empty goals and aimless efforts, never finding the port of peace."

"But the soul who accepts all things as from the Hand of God is already at peace. His wants are My Wants. His will is My Will, which is always the Will of My Father in Heaven. Love, trust, surrender and peace follow in this order. The more Holy Love comes to perfection in your heart, the more you trust—the more you surrender, the more you are at peace."

"You will please make this known."

April 11, 2003
DEEPER LOVE – TRUST – SURRENDER – PEACE
"I am your Jesus, born Incarnate. I invite you to understand that Holy Love, Holy Trust, Holy Surrender and Holy Peace all increase in the soul in proportion to his conformity to the Divine Will. So then, see that as the soul progresses deeper into the Chambers of Our United Hearts—love, trust, surrender and peace become deeper and more profound in his heart, for these are the fruits that conformity to the Divine Will will bear, and Holy Love nourishes them all."

February 14, 2003
PRAY FOR GENUINE PEACE
Jesus is here. He says: "I am your Jesus, born Incarnate."

"I invite souls to understand that peace is the by-product of trust. Trust is your surrender to God's Will in the present moment. The more the soul trusts in himself, the greater the hold evil has on each heart. Pray for genuine peace based on love."

Chastity and Purity

September 21, 2000
VIRTUE OF CHASTITY

"I am God the Father, Creator of Heaven and earth, Creator of Jesus born Incarnate**, Creator of all sexuality."

"I created each soul to pursue chastity, for this is according to My commandments. The human body is created to give life and not lust."

"The virtue of chastity is not one like patience or humility which through time, effort, and grace comes to perfection. No, the chaste soul must always live this virtue perfectly, for any failure in purity is a sin. Like forgiveness, chastity cannot be practiced in portion, but must be observed always."

"As in any virtue, chastity must be observed in thought, word, and deed."

"Each soul has been created to share Heaven with Me. No one reaches the Heart of this Eternal Father through lustful thoughts, words, or actions. These are all inspired by My adversary."

"No one is childlike and at the same time unchaste. It is only the childlike who enter the Kingdom of Heaven."

"Make this known."

**NOTE from Rev. Frank Kenney, S.M., Maureen Sweeney-Kyle's Spiritual Director from 1994-2004:

"According to Pope Paul VI in an address June 30, 1968 on the topic 'The Credo of the People of God' Jesus was 'born of the Father before time began,' and 'through the Father... all things were made' — that is, created, which includes Our Lord's humanity. One birth was from all eternity, impossible for us mortals to totally comprehend, while the other birth happened in time and is well-documented."

September 25, 2000
SATAN'S ATTACKS ON CHASTITY

"I am your Jesus, born Incarnate. My messenger, the way to overcome evil is to uncover it, for as long as the enemy lies under cover of darkness hidden from view, he can flourish. This is how Satan attacks purity of heart:

- Through the media—TV, radio, music, books, pornography, movies;

- By disguising himself as freedom, such as promoting artificial birth control within a marriage as the right to choose;

- By promoting abortions and birth control both in marriage and outside of marriage, making sex an act of enjoyment, and not procreation;

- By labeling homosexuality an alternate life style. It is not. It is a sin.

- By promoting immodest fashions, both male and female. How numerous are the sins committed by giving a bad example or tempting another to unchaste thoughts and desires.

- By compromising consciences to believe that extramarital affairs are acceptable. He does this through the aforementioned media."

"Satan's most profound lie that undermines chastity is that sex was created by God for human enjoyment, not procreation within a marriage. This is why self-will has become the battleground of Satan and his cohorts. If love of self is more important to the soul than love of God and neighbor, Satan has an open door to the heart."

"And so, I invite you to see that unclean spirits come to you every day through these various media and tactics of the adversary, for anything that opposes chastity is an evil spirit. It is up to the human will to unclothe Satan and choose good over evil."

"Make it known."

April 21, 2000 – Good Friday
MEDITATIONS ON THE SORROWFUL MYSTERIES
"I am Jesus, the Word Incarnate...."

THE SCOURGING AT THE PILLAR
"I suffered the mortification of the Scourging for those who commit sins of the flesh."

"...Make all of this known."

Diligence

June 17, 2000
LESSON ON DILIGENCE

"I am your Jesus, born Incarnate. Are you ready for your lesson today? I am here to teach you about the virtue of diligence. Diligence is a virtue much like a container made up of the Will of God in the present moment. Through the practice of diligence, the soul surrenders every present moment task to the Will of God for the love of God. Anything that the soul does which is not done for the love of God is not of eternal value."

"Through the virtue of diligence, the soul performs each task before him as perfectly as possible. But this perfection varies greatly from a worldly perfectionism. The worldly soul wants to perform tasks perfectly to meet with his own satisfaction or the laud of others. The soul who possesses the virtue of diligence takes on each task purely for love of God. Therefore, even the lowliest task is made worthy and holy and gains eternal merit."

"The diligent soul knows well that the present moment will never come again. But every moment can be a part of My Victory through diligence."

"Diligence is like a basket containing freshly baked bread, the bread being the soul's good deeds performed diligently. The aroma of these deeds enhances the environment. The basket is woven of love of God's Will in the present moment."

"Make it known."

June 19, 2000
VIRTUE OF DILIGENCE

"I am your Jesus, born Incarnate. I have come to describe to you the virtue of diligence. Diligence can be likened to the grains of sand in an hourglass. The sand is all the acts performed diligently—that is, for love of God. The hourglass represents the love of God which must embrace every thought, word, and deed in the present moment in order to gain eternal merit. Diligence, more than any other virtue, holds the soul to the present moment. It is through diligence the mundane task is sanctified."

"Make it known."

Meekness

January 15, 1999
LESSON ON MEEKNESS

"Today's lesson is on meekness. I am Jesus, born Incarnate."

"Child, as humility goes hand in hand with love, so meekness is the sister virtue of humility. One can hardly be present, and is present only imperfectly, without the other. Meekness lets the soul attain loftiness. Love is patient and kind. Love is slow to anger. These are all fruits of meekness. Humility of heart allows the virtue of meekness to flower, for it is through humility the soul puts himself last and all others first."

"It is meekness that allows you to be mild in the face of anger—patient in the midst of adversity. Like all virtues, it needs to be in the heart and not superficial. The meek soul treats all people the same—friend and foe alike. The meek soul has his heart in Heaven while on earth. Thus he quickly mounts to perfection."

"Practice meekness. Pray for it. I will adorn your efforts with My grace."

January 23, 2006
ANGER

St. Catherine of Sienna comes. She says: "Praise be to Jesus."

"People these days do not realize the moment to moment warfare they are engaged in. Satan disguises his attacks in many ways. For instance, a soul does not need to lose his temper to cooperate with the spirit of anger. Anger takes on many forms—unforgiveness of self or others, pouting, depression—even procrastination is a form of anger. When the soul cooperates with any of these kindred spirits of anger, he is playing into the hands of Satan."

"Anger, as with any other spirit, is a form of self-love which is inordinate in desire. Self has taken over the center of the heart—replacing love of God and neighbor. This, of course, opposes unity and promotes conflict."

"Remember, as well, when you find fault with your neighbor, you had better look into your own heart with honesty and with courage. Very often the same fault you see in your neighbor is, in fact, a fault you need to work on. Because Satan is a lying spirit, he convinces you it is your neighbor who has such and such a fault."

"Keep your wits about you. Do not let your guard down. Before, you knew nothing of the enemy. Now, you know he is everything that opposes Holy Love in the present moment."

Obedience

April 14, 1999
OBEDIENCE VS. DISOBEDIENCE

Jesus comes in red and white. He says: "I am Jesus, Redeemer and King, born of the flesh. I have come to celebrate with you today this time following My Resurrection. Understand, redemption came to you through My obedience to the cross—the will of the Father."

"So today let us discuss obedience. To understand obedience, first understand disobedience. Disobedience is self-love, for the soul loves his own opinion more than God's opinion, more than the Church's opinion, more than the opinion of his superior that God has placed over him."

"The soul is disobedient that does not obey the commandments. Tantamount to all the commandments is the Law of Holy Love, for it embraces all the others."

"The soul is disobedient that challenges Church law—even if it is in the heart alone. This would include Church dogma, all Church rulings on birth control, women priests, married priests, annulments, forgiveness of sins and My Real Presence in the Eucharist."

"Today there is much confusion about these things. Some judge in the name of discernment. Even My Mother's apparitions are rash-judged. It is not against canon law to visit these sites before they are investigated and found worthy."

"Now let Me tell you about obedience. When you obey those in authority over you, you are always accomplishing God's Holy and Divine Will. Obedience is like the sail of a ship, which carried along on the breeze of self-surrender sails safely into port. Or it is like the shoe on your foot which goes where the will directs it. Obedience is a refuge—a mantle of grace. It is a shadow of the soul's humility. It is difficult for the proud to be obedient."

"Come to Me and I will assist you in this and all the virtues. I love you. I will bless you."

May 8, 2000
OBEY THE DIVINE WILL

Jesus and Blessed Mother are here. Their Hearts are exposed. Blessed Mother says: "Praise be to Jesus."

Jesus: "I am your Jesus, born Incarnate. Tonight I have come to help you realize that when you surrender to the Divine Will in the present moment, you are surrendering to your own holiness. Obeying the Divine Will means to accept everything as from the Hand of God, understanding that grace will provide. Tonight We're extending to you the Blessing of Our United Hearts."

January 27, 2002
OBEY THE COMMANDMENTS –
THE MAGISTERIUM – ALL CHURCH LAW

Jesus is here with His Heart exposed. He says: "I am your Jesus, born Incarnate."

"My brothers and sisters, the depth of your belief in this Holy Love Message is reflected in your thoughts, words and deeds. If you truly believe, then you will obey all of the commandments, for this Law of Love embraces all of the commandments. Further, if you are Catholic, you will be obedient to the Magisterium and all Church law, and you will reverence My Real Presence in the Blessed Sacrament. My coming to you is not your salvation, My brothers and sisters. Listen and live the Message."

"I'm extending to you My Blessing of Divine Love."

January 9, 2006
LISTEN TO THOSE YOU SHOULD OBEY

Jesus and Blessed Mother are here with Their Hearts exposed. Blessed Mother says: "Praise be to Jesus." Jesus says: "I am your Jesus, born Incarnate."

Jesus: "My brothers and sisters, I have come to help you along the path of Holy and Divine Love. Always place God in the center of your hearts, and with this love, serve others faithfully. This will lead you deeper into love, humility and simplicity. Do not be attached to your own agendas or opinions, but listen especially to those to whom you should be obeying."

Patience

February 3, 1999
LOVE, HUMILITY AND PATIENCE

The Sacred Heart of Jesus appears. Jesus smiles. He says: "I am Jesus, born Incarnate. Please transcribe this."

"Love is patient. Yes, it is true. Patience so closely follows Holy Love—Holy Humility. It is the virtue that reflects love and humility more than any other. Patience is the fruit of love and humility which allows the soul to unite to the Cross. Where patience is lacking you find a flaw in love and humility."

"If Holy Love was a delicious soup, the broth would be patience flavored by the ingredients of love and humility."

"Patience is like a sand castle built by the sea, the sand being love and humility. It takes human effort to construct the castle. Thus you must, with your will, turn your hearts over to patience. Do not allow your efforts in this virtue to be washed away through self-love."

"My grace and blessing will combine with your efforts. Pray for this virtue. It is the reflection of holiness."

September 27, 2001
PATIENCE VS. IMPATIENCE

"I am your Jesus, born Incarnate. I love when you think of Me and turn your heart over to Me. Yes, let Me be your portion, your provision. Revere our time together, as I do."

Maureen: "Jesus, what do I need to overcome in order to go deeper into Your Heart?"

Jesus: "Impatience is a sign of a weak point in humility and love. I ask you to be able to bear all things patiently for love of Me. Did I not do so for you? Do not listen to Satan when he starts to suggest others' weak points. You will know it is Me speaking to you of others by the peace in your heart. When Satan criticizes others to you, his goal is to agitate you."

"When you fast, let it be from your own will. You can accomplish much change in this type of fast."

"I am revealing to you the Kingdom of My Divine Heart. Treasure what I tell you in love."

September 30, 2002
IMITATE BLESSED MOTHER'S PATIENCE

Mary of Agreda comes. She says: "Praise be to Jesus. My sister, take this down."

"I am here to speak to you about the virtue of patience in the life of the Blessed Virgin Mary. Our Lady, who was perfect in every virtue, never allowed time to become Her enemy. In this way She never thought about the past in a negative context—nor did She worry over the future. This allowed Her to patiently live out the present moment in patience and humility. She did not consider how many times She performed a simple task in the past or how long She would need to wait for something in the future. She did not fault others for their sins—thus showing impatience with them. Instead, She prayed for them."

"When She saw Her Son suffer She did not have a bitter Heart, but was patient with God's Will for Her and Jesus in the present moment. She endured patiently every separation from Jesus—even His Ascent into Heaven."

"Humility and love were the basis of Her patience, and they shone through Her like sun shines through crystal."

"Imitate Her."

October 21, 2005
PATIENTLY AWAIT DIVINE PROVISION

Jesus is here with His Heart exposed and says: "I am your Jesus, born Incarnate."

"My brothers and sisters, I have come to remind you that it is the humble heart that is most easily given over to patience. It is only with great patience that you can await Heaven's Provision. Everyone who awaits some type of Divine Provision, whether it is a particular grace, a conversion of a family member or guidance along the path of holiness—each one must practice humility and patience as you await what Heaven offers. Do not jump to conclusions. Wait on My Provision, and I will show you where to go, what to do, when to speak and when to be silent."

"Tonight I'm blessing you with My Blessing of Divine Love."

November 24, 2005
PATIENCE AND LONG-SUFFERING

"I am your Jesus, born Incarnate."

"This is how we must do everything—together. Invite Me along in the least little effort. Be patient. Patience bears the fruit of long-suffering."

Prudence and Discernment

March 5, 1998
LET PRUDENCE STAND GUARD

Jesus and Blessed Mother come together. Their Hearts are exposed. Blessed Mother says: "Praised be Jesus. I have come to invite My children to integrate Holy Love into their daily lives."

Jesus says: "Let Holy Prudence stand guard over your senses and every thought, word, and deed."

"Tonight We are extending to you the Blessing of the United Hearts."

January 19, 2000
LESSON ON PRUDENCE

"I am your Jesus, born Incarnate. I have come to help you understand the virtue of prudence. Prudence is the conscience of your soul. The prudent person lets Holy Love stand guard over his thoughts, words, and actions. Prudence is like a watchdog which guards his territory against marauders. Prudence stands guard over the soul, monitoring its motives and actions."

"If prudence could be seen, it would be like a sieve—filtering out all that is evil and keeping what is good. Or if prudence could be tasted, it would be like salt which enhances what it touches and makes it more perfect—more palatable."

"The soul cannot make himself prudent, just as food cannot season itself. But the soul can practice prudence and pray for it. Sincerity and simplicity precede prudence of heart. They ready the heart for prudence to enter. Prudence comes to perfection in wisdom. But every virtue has its root in love."

May 9, 2000
LESSON ON PRUDENCE *(PART 1)*

"I am your Jesus, born Incarnate. I have come to help you understand the virtue of prudence. In prudence, wisdom and simplicity are combined. It is prudence which regulates our thoughts, word, and actions. Do you speak too much or not enough? Are you prone to excess in your actions or use of time? Do you allow Satan to rob you of the present by excessive thoughts of the past or future?"

"The prudent person understands his own heart. He prudently avoids temptations and excesses."

May 13, 2000
LESSON ON PRUDENCE *(PART 2)*

"I am your Jesus, born Incarnate. I have come today to help you understand the virtue of prudence. The first rule of prudence is righteousness—that is, obedience to God's commandments. Prudence dictates the avoidance of excess in thought, word, or deed. A soul may be wise, but still lack prudence. For instance, a wise soul may—in trying to make a point—state his view over and over, not knowing when enough has been said. This shows lack of trust in My grace. I'll tell you why. This type of soul makes his point, but is unwilling to state his case and [then] let grace do the rest. He cannot allow grace to carry the point into the heart. He seems to think everything depends on his efforts."

"Prudence governs all the virtues. Sometimes we do not prudently use the virtues. Sometimes a person is too patient and does not speak up in the face of wrong. Or he may show love by spoiling a child and giving in to the child excessively."

"Prudence is not synonymous with self-righteousness either. For the prudent person seeks to know himself better, searches out his weaknesses and works on them. The simple-hearted soul has little difficulty with prudence, but the proud-hearted find this virtue elusive."

February 19, 2000
LESSON ON DISCERNMENT

"I am your Jesus, born Incarnate. Today, I have come to discuss with you the topic of discernment. Discernment is a gift of the Holy Spirit which follows the virtues of prudence and wisdom. It is deeper than these two and can be likened to instinct in nature. Animals, birds, and fish are born with instincts which help them survive in the wild. These instincts also dictate behavioral patterns such as the swallows' return to Capistrano every year."

"In the spiritual realm, discernment is a necessity in distinguishing good from evil. Many never obtain the depth of this virtue. They mistake evil for good and vice versa. Discernment—to be real—comes from deep within the soul. It cannot be fingered or indexed. It is a feeling from within. It is not unlike viewing several fine paintings, but feeling from within that one is better than all the rest because it is painted in a more skillful, masterly way."

"Discernment mounts from many spiritual experiences. There is danger then, when someone presumes they have discernment because they have other gifts, or thinks they have other gifts. Many have been led astray in this way. Many who should have this gift, because they are in positions of authority, do not."

"Discernment is not synonymous with authority. It is not rash judgment based on leaping to conclusions. It is an opinion based on sifting out the truth from falsehood. It is like a ship's compass holding the vessel on course. Discernment keeps your soul on track of good."

"This is a rare gift, given with love and care by God to the humble-hearted."

"You will make this known."

January 2, 2001
TRUE VS. FALSE DISCERNMENT

"I am your Jesus, born Incarnate. My messenger, know and understand this. True discernment does not come through the intellect. It is a gift I place in the heart. Just as with any virtue, there can be a false imitator of the true virtue. In discernment this is recognized as pharisaical interpretation of the truth. False discernment is easily accepted by a person who depends on his own intellect for answers instead of the Holy Spirit. Such a one may pride himself on his intellect and/or his virtue."

"The truth of what I reveal here bears the responsibility of making it known."

August 3, 2005
TRUE GIFT OF DISCERNMENT

St. Thomas Aquinas comes. He says: "Praise be to Jesus."

"I have come to further describe to you the true gift of discernment. Many proclaim this gift, feign this gift, presume to have this gift. These are the ones to beware of. These are the ones who, in reality, have only spiritual pride."

"True discernment is like a gourmet palate which, when introduced to a fine wine, recognizes and appreciates the depth and richness of it. The gourmet does not make a snap judgment. Rather, he savors the wine slowly, allowing it to interact with the sensitive taste buds—a gift God has given him. There is nothing superficial about the conclusion he draws concerning the wine. He does not base his conclusion on preconceived opinions, but on the experience of his own interaction with the wine."

"How true this is in regard to spiritual discernment. So often pride is the judge, and the gift of discernment is not even present. Messages from Heaven must touch the soul. They must interact with the spirit. Like fine wine, they must be savored—their essence felt before a conclusion is drawn."

"So much damage is done by those who proclaim faulty discernment. It is an important tool in the hands of Satan—a tool he uses freely to destroy much of Heaven's work. It is only through pride he can succeed in this."

"Peoples' opinions are not the same as the gift of discernment, though they may be presented as such. Beware!"

The United Hearts
of
Jesus and Mary